FIRE&
FRAGRANCE

SEAN FEUCHT & ANDY BYRD

FIRE&
FRAGRANCE

FROM THE GREAT COMMANDMENT
TO THE GREAT COMMISSION

DESTINY IMAGE® PUBLISHERS, INC.
P.O. Box 310, Shippensburg, PA 17257-0310
"Speaking to the Purposes of God for This Generation and for the Generations to Come."

This book and all other Destiny Image, Revival Press, MercyPlace, Fresh Bread, Destiny Image Fiction, and Treasure House books are available at Christian bookstores and distributors worldwide.

For a U.S. bookstore nearest you, call 1-800-722-6774.
For more information on foreign distributors, call 717-532-3040.
Or reach us on the Internet: www.destinyimage.com.

Trade Paper ISBN 13: 978-0-7684-3290-9
Hardcover ISBN 13: 978-0-7684-3469-9
Large Print ISBN 13: 978-0-7684-3470-5
Ebook ISBN 13: 978-0-7684-9078-7

For Worldwide Distribution, Printed in the U.S.A.
2 3 4 5 6 7 8 / 14 13 12 11 10

DEDICATION

I would like to dedicate this book to my father and missions pioneer, Christopher Feucht. I humbly follow the rich heritage and legacy you have passed down. I long await the day I see you again in eternity. Also, to my gorgeous wife and the glory girl of promise you are carrying. I love you both immensely. —Sean

First, I would like to dedicate this book to my parents, Vernon and Valerie Byrd. I don't think that two parents have believed in their sons more! Second, to you, my inspiring and stunning wife, Holly, and to our three little burning ones, Asher, Hadassah, and Rhema. May your fires burn so much brighter than mine! —Andy

Together, we would like to honor all the fathers and mothers, in Heaven and on Earth, who fought the battles, spilled their blood, cried their tears, and paved the way for a generation to live in these unprecedented times.

ENDORSEMENTS

The leaders who move history give articulation to that which is already silently rumbling in the collective conscience of the masses. When that articulated word is released, bones rattle and great people movements begin to shake the earth. My friend Sean Feucht is one of those leaders. The gift of God upon him has kindled a flame that a generation created to praise, pray, and practice justice in the earth is lighting their candle to, and the lamp of that Burn is lighting the world. The young man's story is truly a sign and a wonder in the nations. Don't read this book if you don't want to be a burning man or a burning woman.

Lou Engle
Co-founder and president, TheCall
Kansas City, Missouri

This is a great book by a great guy with a great message. It is a timely word for those seeking to live lives of convergence: between

Heaven and earth, between sacred and secular, between nations, and between the movements of prayer and mission. Get it, read it, and help spread the virus!

Pete Greig
24-7 Prayer and Alpha International
London, England

Sean's book reveals that worship is our greatest tool and weapon in the Kingdom. There is an atmospheric shift that takes place in the earthly realm when we worship our Creator. This book shows us firsthand how the fire and presence of Heaven can bring a supernatural impartation enabling us to spread the fragrance everywhere we go! Thanks, Sean!

Beni Johnson
Prayer Pastor at Bethel Church, Redding, California
Author of *The Happy Intecessor*

If you would like a glimpse of the future of world missions, read on! From Eternity Past into the endlessness of the Future Kingdom, God's relentless, jealous pursuit of the heart of man is the story of all ages. It fuels our burning passion for His Presence, our worship, and our missions. Sean and Andy are the real deal, heralds of a new model and a final phase of world evangelization. Read this book and get ready for the next 10 to 20 years as "musicianaries" introduce the sounds of Heaven to nation after nation, from the rising of the sun to the going down of the same!

Charles Stock
Senior pastor, Life Center Ministries International
Harrisburg, Pennsylvania

Sean Feucht is a revolutionary leader who is helping to define the DNA of a new movement in Christianity. I have been watching his life and what he is raising up through his calling of worship, intercession, missions, and revival, and I am so excited about this book because it's a representation of that very life he is living. It is a call to action, and it's a call for you!

Shawn Bolz
Senior pastor, Expression58, Hollywood, California
Author of *Keys to Heaven's Economy* and
The Throne Room Company

The search for the face of God ends with a revelation of His love for all humankind. Out of the encounter with His Presence is birthed a compelling love for the whole world, and an automatic desire to give everything to see His desire fulfilled (see John 17:24). Sean and Andy have both touched this fire and gone to the nations, so they speak with authority to a new breed in the final frontiers of the global missions movement. *Fire and Fragrance* will cause you to burn with the same passion that motivated Jesus to leave His Kingdom for earth. It is a dangerous read—if taken seriously, it will change your life.

Wesley and Stacey Campbell
RevivalNOW! Ministries and *Be A Hero*
Kelowna, British Columbia

It's a joy to endorse my dear friend Andy Byrd's co-authorship of this book, *Fire and Fragrance*, because I know the intrinsic worth of his character. This man writes out of his consistent passionate relationship with the living Christ. The contents throb with vitality and challenge because Andy is making God's priorities his priorities. This book gives us insights into the fire of God's glory. I love it.

Joy Dawson
Tuyunga, California
P.S. It may be too hot for some!

The first time I taught on worship evangelism was in Pittsburgh in 1983. During the teaching I stated that "God would release a 'musicianary' movement that would shake nations with the sound of His heart." I believe that the shaking has begun. To see "musicianaries" like Sean now rising up with the sound and vocabulary of God's heart excites me beyond words.

Ray Hughes
Selah Ministries
Nashville, Tennessee
Author of *The Minstrel Series*

One cannot read Sean Feucht and Andy Byrd's *Fire and Fragrance* without becoming passionately in love with God. It tears apart complacency until it is shattered and fuels a passion to see the nations worship our King. This is a much-needed book as God loves the world (John 3:16) as well as individuals. The good news is that a burning heart will never leave you anything but consumed by God—and it absolutely torches the devil!

Cindy Jacobs
Generals International
Dallas, Texas

In every generation God raises up voices who not only instruct His people but call them to live radically abandoned to the cause of Christ on the earth. Sean Feucht is one of those voices. God is using Sean to release the cry for revival in the nations of the world, and a movement of worship, prayer, and missions is arising that is full of fire. It is not just a movement of events or gatherings but is genuinely birthed in the hearts of believers who, in pursuing the presence of God, are becoming the fulfillment of their prayers. Sean not only has the anointing to call a generation to live wholeheartedly before the Lord, but he has the anointing to impart this lifestyle because of His own hunger and passion for God and global revival.

Banning Liebscher
Jesus Culture director
Redding, California
Author of *Jesus Culture: Living a Life That Transforms the World*

In every generation there arises new, fresh voices that speak to their times, their peers, and even to nations. Sean Feucht with Burn 24-7 is one of those penetrating voices crying out in the wilderness to make a way for the Lord. Your faith will be stirred to a flame as you read the testimonies of one who believes in the pursuit of God's presence with radical abandonment. Let your heart burn warmly within as you partner with Sean and others to win for the Lamb the rewards of His sufferings.

James W. Goll
Encounters Network, Prayer Storm, Compassion Acts
Franklin, Tennessee
Author of *The Seer*, *The Lost Art of Intercession*, *Praying for Israel's Destiny*, and many more

PREMISE

The premise of this book is to cast vision and give language to a generation to live in the confluence of the global missions and prayer movements, to hunger for the fullness of God, and to live a lifestyle that can release and sustain global revival and reformation.

TABLE OF CONTENTS

FOREWORD

This book is like turning on God's GPS unit to discover His direction and destiny for this generation. Read it and devour its message. It will draw you into God's presence and into a fulfillment of your deepest longings for your sense of place and belonging. It will also inspire you to drive full-speed ahead into both a local and global (a "glocal") transforming movement with your peers...followers of none other than Jesus Christ.

Like the supersonic jet breaking the sound barrier, the sound of revival is following Jesus as He initiates a new movement at warp speeds across the earth. He's amplifying the sound of healing, revival, and ministry to those imprisoned by addictions, fear, unbelief, and injustice—those who are rejected, trafficked...those experiencing any and all afflictions that demonic arsenals can muster. The wrath of Jesus against the enemy is being unleashed with the greatest fury in history.

The Holy Spirit is responding by launching two strategic and crucial movements: the worship movement, with its refrains rising to a crescendo unlike anything known in more than a century, and the prayer movement, which has been exploding among youth at an unprecedented level. Millions of young people are participating in the Global Prayer Day and thousands are plugging into houses of prayer across the United States, the "furnaces" of Europe, and around the world. Mobile prayer troubadours are also arising, such as Lou Engle with "TheCall" and Sean Feucht, leading the movement of worship, praise, and prayer with "Burn 24-7." These movements are fueling the raging inferno of impending revival and boldly announcing the move of God among this digital/instantaneous-minded generation worldwide. The timing is perfect.

The societal and technological factors fueling this revival are many: The world is more connected than ever before because of the ease of international travel, the Internet, widespread wireless use, and the social networking phenomenon that connects us in ever-tightening circles. The mind-set, heart-set, and available technologies are all drawing us closer to this revival. For the first time, you can travel to nearly anywhere on the planet within a matter of hours. You can talk with your friends 24/7 from anywhere to anywhere.

Jesus said, "Go into all the world…." Jets have conquered the geographical barrier that once separated us. He said, "Preach the Gospel to every creature…." Communication and information technologies have made it possible to do this very thing. Like the stones in David's sling in the battle against Goliath, the practical means of the completion of the great commission are available and ready to strike at the "head of the serpent." Therefore, satan's hold on the earth is about to get crushed!

The final "surprise of God" to shock hell and bring rejoicing in Heaven is the seamless unity and convergence of all these tools and movements with the global missions movement. I am witnessing the physical manifestation of the vision of God I received while still a young man: waves of young people covering the earth. What was unheard of 50 years ago (young people as a missions force) is now common. But what is uncommon is the birth of movements such as Call2All Next Generation, which are catching fire around the world. These are just a foreshadowing of what is yet to come.

Sean Feucht, a psalmist and pioneer, has teamed up with Youth With A Mission leader Andy Byrd in writing *Fire and Fragrance*. They are a youthful duo who are living out authentically the message that they speak. With great passion, they are seeking and finding intimacy with God. In coming to know the depths of God, they are desiring to make Him known in breadth throughout the world. They are doing it!

Loren Cunningham
Kona, Hawaii
Founder, Youth With A Mission
President, University of the Nations International

INTRODUCTION

For 2,000 years, the Kingdom of God has been moving forward in one increasing apostolic thrust after another. In many ways, these thrusts could be likened to a wave that continues to crash upon the shores of our planet, working its way to every last human heart, geographical area, and sphere of society. This wave of God is broad, encompassing a much wider expression of the Kingdom than any one person or organization or denomination could carry. Within this wave are all of the answers for a dying, lost world and a challenge to move into the Edenic purposes of God for the earth. Revival, reformation, and restoration are at the very center of the heart of God for this planet as He prepares it for the return of His Son.

As the apostolic wave continues its move across the earth, God raises up prophetic signposts to remind us of forgotten or neglected aspects of His holistic Kingdom. In the 1500s it was the restoration of the priesthood of all believers. In the 1600s God restored an individual's choice to be baptized and follow God. In the 1700s the missions movement was relaunched among the Moravians, resulting in a global missions movement still in existence. In the 1800s liberty became the absolute outflow of the Gospel as Wilberforce and many others sought to reform society through the abolishment of slavery. Also in the 1800s, biblical education laid a foundation for the Gospel to spread into every sphere of society as the Gospel became the foundation for entire nations and governments. In the early 1900s God raised up the healing revivals to remind the global Body of His heart to heal the body and the soul.

None of these "prophetic words" were the apostolic thrust in and of themselves, but all were clear signposts to the global Bride of the heart of God and the solution for their hour of human history. As the Body walks together, heeding the prophetic signposts, an element of fullness is released into the global Bride and the appropriate response for the appropriate times releases great measures of the Kingdom of God!

In this day, God is declaring from His heavenly throne, *"My house will be called a house of prayer for all nations"* (Mark 11:17). The Church has always prayed to one degree or another, and what is being called the "prayer movement" is not the sole expression of the Kingdom, but rather a timely prophetic word to the Body of Christ. His Presence must be the solution. His Presence must be the primary aim of every believer. His glory is most released when His Presence is most adored! His Presence is the very essence of this global wave of the Kingdom that has been crashing on the earth for 2,000 years. In this hour God is teaching us once again how to live and practice His Presence as it becomes our consuming passion in all of life! The language is prayer, the rhythm is worship, the passion is intercession, and the outflow is radical exploits of evangelism! A marriage of missions and prayer is returning the Church to its New Testament roots and foundations.

The heart of this book is to be a prophetic word released into the hearts of all who read it. This global trumpet blast to return to our first love is what God is using to bring the church back into alignment. In this book we are not attempting to cover all the various ways that the apostolic wave of the Kingdom has moved or is moving, but rather to prop up a signpost in the middle of all we do that would cry out for His Presence. From that addiction to His Presence we are called to become the very fragrance of Christ to a world in great need! In no way do we desire to devalue any of the many expressions of the Kingdom and many aspects of this apostolic wave but rather to add value to all of them through this global signpost! We cannot afford not to hear what God is saying in this hour of salvation history. By hearing His voice and agreeing with Him, we discover the very key to unlocking the greatest harvest of souls in human history and the greatest shining glory the Church has ever walked in!

1

A DAY LIKE NO OTHER

It was an arid and clear night when we descended toward a small town located in the desert of Northern Iraq. As the wheels touched the tarmac at 3 A.M., my (Sean's) heart began to beat with excitement, anticipation, and wonder at what God was about to do in the following hours and days with our team. We had recently begun to partner with a beautiful young couple God strategically planted in that region to raise up a furnace of unending worship and prayer, releasing the indigenous sound of adoration from where justice, mercy, and supernatural outreach can flow across the barren land.

Ever since Adam walked intimately "in the cool of the day" with the Lord in the Garden of Eden thousands of years ago, God has set in motion a divine strategy to beckon His Bride back to that place of communion and oneness with Him. This plan of redemption and restoration is unfolding all over the world as millions of souls are being drawn back to that place of awakening, salvation, and desire for the Father. In the very same geographical region where that intimacy in the Garden was first displayed and revealed to humanity, modern-day Iraq is experiencing a wave of restoration and salvation. Since the collapse and removal of Saddam Hussein and his agenda of genocide against the Kurdish peoples, the gateway to the cities and hearts of these un-reached Muslims has been opened wide for further reception to the Good News of salvation.

At the same time I was collecting my bags and walking through customs, our team was gathered in an underground Iranian house church 30 kilometers away, burning their flame of love through the night with hungry Kurdish believers from across the region. I left directly from the airport to join them in their sound and pursuit. Our Burn 24-7 mission trips are packed full of intensity and adventure, and it is not uncommon for us to organize and mobilize four to five strategic nonstop strikes of 24-hour worship, prayer, and outreach in several different cities on one trip. That night was marked by boisterous worship sets where songs and prayers in English, Kurdish, and Iraqi mingled together in one unique, yet beautiful, fragrance flooding out into the streets of the city.

Just a few days earlier, high-ranking government officials were walking through and examining a primary school where our team was worshiping while English lessons were being given. We have noticed that as we use worship in conjunction with tools of outreach, miracles and breakthrough seems to follow us every step of the way! The officials were overwhelmed as they took in the scene of musicians and singers pouring out their hearts to God. After a few hours of watching this unfold, they approached our team and remarked: "We don't know why we came here or who you are, but this sound we hear is healing music for our nation." Then, they invited us to gather in a few days to play this "healing music" at the old military fortress and nearby northern palace of Saddam Hussein. We had to have them repeat this offer a few times as we could barely believe what our ears heard!

A few days later, and after some serious prayer, impressions, and dreams confirming we were to walk through this open door, we ventured out into the desert near the Iran-Iraq border toward the compound. None of us could have comprehended what was in store that day. God was about to transform a former stronghold of death, fear, and intimidation against the Kurdish people into a resting place of His Presence. The fragrance of worship was going to rise and the sound of life, hope, restoration, and salvation released!

Upon our arrival, the leaders began to share with us the history of the fortress. From this place strategies were birthed, developed, and executed through Saddam and his top officials that condemned the lives of thousands of Kurdish people through the unleashing of biological weapons. Conservative estimates place the death toll at over 200,000 Kurdish people murdered through genocide over the past ten years in northern Iraq. On our drive to the palace, we passed entire towns and villages that were literally erased from existence in mere seconds by these weapons. Out of the ashes of one of the worst human tragedies of our lifetime, an authentic move of God is taking place in this nation, and it is being birthed from the place of extravagant worship and prayer!

Following the end of a quick tour of the palace and compound, we entered into the main gathering room and were greeted with the elated smiles of hundreds of Kurdish Muslim men, women, and children waiting with great expectancy. You could feel the weight of their eagerness in the room as they giggled and gave quick, nervous glances. The sight of them almost immediately brought me to tears. God had literally ushered us into the former king's lair of the nation and provided a captive audience of some of the most unreached people on the planet. They were also welcoming us to play "healing music"! The days we are living in are unlike any in history and divinely ridiculous situations like this are constant reminders that are becoming rather common. They are scenarios and circumstances that no human can possibly orchestrate as we humbly follow the wind of the Holy Spirit. The story only gets better from here!

As we began to set up our guitars and hand drums, I noticed there were three very nice professional cameras strategically placed around the room. I asked one of the leaders what these cameras were for and if they planned to film that night. He told me that they wanted to give those who could not fit into the small room the opportunity to hear and experience the music. I then assumed it was for those Kurds who lived in the surrounding villages and towns, until he motioned for me to follow him through the back door of the building; I beheld several massive, gigantic satellite dishes. They were easily comparable to those you would see at major news network headquarters. The explanation was then given that this was the base site of the national Kurdish television station seen by an estimated 20 to 25 million Kurds scattered across Iraq, Iran, Turkey, Syria, and even into the West who tune in every night.

Apparently, this station was the Kurds' main source of information on weather, news, and updates from the newly established government base in northern Iraq. He told me that during that night's program, millions of viewers across the world would be pleasantly surprised to see and hear Americans playing music on this station for the first time in history. At this point in our conversation, my mouth was wide open and would not shut. God immediately reminded me of a prophetic word spoken over me almost a year prior. The word echoed in my mind and spoke of how God would supernaturally broadcast the raw, lovesick sound from the Burn 24-7 movement to the most unreached people groups of the world. At the time, it seemed like a lofty word that would take years to come true. God brought this word into literal fulfillment that night! This is a perfect testimony revealing the days of rapid acceleration that are upon us! What once took years to accomplish is now taking months and what used to take months is now coming to pass in mere days!

From the strum of the very first chord that night, the beautiful Presence of God rushed into the room eager to respond to the resonating cry of worship and ready to meet the needs of the lost. We were ushered into a realm of heavenly vertical worship and blatantly and intentionally went after His face with reckless abandon! We prophesied through our songs and prayers and released declarations over the nation of Iraq, the Kurdish people scattered across the world, and the millions of listeners tuning in. The Kurdish Muslims in the room had never seen anything like it, but the experience absolutely captivated them! They were drawn in and jumped into our expression of love to God by singing, clapping, and even dancing! I have never experienced such openness and reception before with a totally unreached people group. Worship prepares the way!

At one point during the three-hour televised burn set, during a crazy drum circle, everyone was unified in the traditional Kurdish dance as we sang the spontaneous song of the Lord. It was completely wild, free, and unpredictable—and God was in our midst! The Presence of God was enjoyed and the people well received that night, as the entire climate of that compound shifted from fear to love, sorrow to joy, and anxiety to peace. The atmosphere of worship and prayer cultivated space for the kiss of Heaven to reach broken humanity. Many of these unreached Muslims were radically and immediately healed from disease, pain, and sickness as we began to pray and sing over them. The grand highlight and most beautiful fruit was the lost souls who surrendered their very lives to Jesus from the encounter. It felt like a homecoming celebration, and we could not stop rejoicing for the faithfulness of the Father to visit these gorgeous people. It was one of the most epic worship services of all time!

Unlike Any Other

This story is one of many accounts in our day revealing the hour of visitation, encounter, acceleration, and salvation that is already upon us! This entire book could easily be filled with captivating testimonies on this level and beyond, as these moments mark the glory of the Lord rising in new dimensions on His sons and daughters, as promised throughout Scripture. (See Numbers 14:21, Psalm 72:19, Isaiah 6:3, and Habakkuk 2:14.) The Gospel of the Kingdom is forcefully advancing and exploding across the darkest and hardest nations of the world as the lost become awestruck with the beauty, power, and majesty of the Person of God. The place of encounter is drawing them in.

The wave of this global momentum is now peaking among the nations of the Far East. China, India, and Nepal are experiencing awesome moves of God and a massive harvest of souls unheard of in history. This cyclone of fire is beginning to expand westward, through central Asia and the Middle East en route to Jerusalem, where the final showdown of the earth will take place. Muslims, Hindus, and Buddhists are coming to Jesus in droves, and the sustaining fruit from their truly transformed lives is shifting culture in their cities, regions, and nations.

A recent study that took place at the University of the Nations on the Youth With A Mission (YWAM) base in Kona, Hawaii, accurately articulated and depicted this current happening. Some of Christendom's most brilliant minds gathered and compiled data from the largest missions and outreach organizations in the world with the focus of tracking the rate of evangelism among the least reached peoples of the earth. A discovery was made that if the global Church continues on the current level of outreach, evangelism, and missions without even gaining momentum—which has been growing every year—every nation, tribe, and tongue would hear the Gospel by the year 2020. Worship and prayer provide a massive catalyst of this movement as the sound of adoration, praise, and thanksgiving is being released all over the earth like never before! The declaration in Malachi 1:11 is literally coming into fulfillment and is bearing the fruit of authentic salvation on the earth:

> *"My name will be great among the nations, from the rising to the setting of the sun. In every place incense and pure offerings will be brought to My name, because My name will be great among the nations," says the Lord Almighty* (Malachi 1:11 NIV).

This prophetic promise is already underway as the chorus of billions of burning hearts from across the nations of the world is joining with the mighty throng in Heaven proclaiming the greatness of God! Incense is being released and flooding the earth as more cities than ever before are burning with this flame that continues day and night!

We also must look to the biblical blueprint from Psalm 67:5-7, where we observe what directly follows this global release of incense!

> *May the peoples praise You, O God; may all the peoples praise You. Then the land will yield its harvest, and God, our God, will bless us. God will bless us, and all the ends of the earth will fear Him* (Psalm 67:5-7 NIV).

The largest global harvest in history will come directly on the heels of the extravagant sound of love, adoration, and praise that is released from the blazing Bride. The worldwide billion-soul harvest that has been spoken of, dreamed of, and prophesied by many leaders across the Body in the past ten years is quickly approaching. We are going to witness firsthand the beautiful correlation between the fire ignited in our hearts and the release of the fragrance and aroma of Christ on the earth.

The Presence Community

Imagine communities all over the earth where the priority of life was cultivating, enjoying, and releasing the presence of God. Communities whose life, direction, and impact were all based in a furnace of prayer, soaking, worship, and intercession. Imagine these communities burning so bright that they began to emanate the very glory of God that they so lovingly, endearingly, and consistently gazed upon. Imagine the impact on some of the darkest, hardest, most closed, and most complacent regions of the world as these communities began to walk in the fullness of a marriage of radical devotion to ministering to the heart of the Lord with a burning passion to take Jesus to the streets, the orphanages, the slums, the remote villages, the red light districts, urban centers, suburbs, and every sphere of society. What would be possible if these communities began to come together around a shared value for both the personal, manifest presence of God and His longing and desire to take His Presence to the streets: the enjoyment and release of His Presence. The monastic and the missional, intimacy and advocacy, communion and commissioning, gazing and going, fire and fragrance! Some of these communities would live together; others would regularly gather; all would be influencing spheres of society, living in the breakthrough of the victorious Bride and releasing it everywhere they go.

Would change be possible with and through these communities? Could darkness experience light? Could the church live in love and power, and release love with power? Could a generation of young people awaken to their destinies? Could injustice be thwarted, morality restored, and true liberty released? Has the darkness of the predawn ever been able to hold back the first rays of the morning sun? Has a dark room ever pushed back against the force of light sent by the flipping of a switch and the illumination of a bulb? So what is missing? Light? Switches? Faith?

The Dawning of a New Day

It does not take a prophet or a prophetic word to clearly see that the Western church is struggling as much as ever with how to maintain a vibrant spiritual life while being salt and light to a world filled with darkness. Anyone who can read has plenty of reasons to be discouraged with sliding morals, demonic laws, and increasingly humanistic ideals celebrated worldwide. However, it takes a totally different kind of person, operating in a different perspective, bringing a different reality, to see all of this and yet live with a constant, confident hope that the

Kingdom of God will not be stopped, and despite the headlines of the media, He is winning!

What is His strategy for change? How will we turn this thing around? How will we fulfill the declaration of Jesus that we are *"the light of the world"* (Matt. 5:14)?

Hope. Hope is what we need. Hope in a Heaven that has never lost a battle in the long run but only knows breakthroughs and coming breakthroughs! Hope that when Jesus said that the gates of hell could not prevail against His Church, He really meant it. So what is missing? Church? True, fiery, intimate, impacting communities gazing at glory, being transformed into glory, and being the fulfillment of the glory of God covering the earth as the waters cover the seas! We have to begin to dream again. We must awaken to the possibilities and not be consumed with the limitations, temporary setbacks, or difficult circumstances. It is time to come fully alive.

What needs to change? Everything! We have settled for so little. We have given the Lamb a short and sweet Sunday morning gathering as the reward of His suffering. *Radical* has been defined as loud, big, or unique. Devotion has been relegated to a loose set of dos and do nots. But, oh, there is hope! There is so much hope. This Bride will awaken, will rise up, and will walk in the fullness of her destiny. All throughout history there has been a fiery remnant and our day is no different. The uniqueness of our day is going to be the breadth and width of this fire-filled army. Communities can be transformed, the lost can be reached, the hardest heart can soften, the most addicted can experience liberty, and our nations can turn their hearts back to God. We must live in hope; we must live in the breakthrough. Anything less is to scorn our inheritance and to cheapen the victory that was won on Calvary.

The Cry for Fullness

In this endeavor we believe God is releasing a cry of desperation in hungry hearts all over the world that will never be satisfied with the status quo. Fullness is the true cry of a generation! The solutions to this earth's problems cannot be summed up on white boards; their answers will not be solved by the greatest attempts of our humanistic governments or our new church programs. The Presence of God is the only answer! It always has been the only answer, but it is as if we are awakening to that reality more and more.

Fire cannot burn without fragrance being released, and you cannot have the fragrance of smoke without first starting a fire. The fire of passionate, zealous love for Jesus has always been the foundation of the fragrance of Christ impacting the spheres of society, nations, and the entire globe in a truly Kingdom-building way. God is calling His Church to enter into the "burning hearts" of those who walked the road to Emmaus (see Luke 24:32). From this fire, fragrance will naturally be released. The fragrance of a burning heart is the greatest evangelism scent the world has ever smelled. That fragrance will manifest as supernatural, merciful, compassionate, practical, influential, societal, nonreligious, and ultimately transformational! Raw passion for a raw God impacting a raw society with the raw Gospel! No more pasteurization of the Gospel, no more processed intimacy with a refined God! Raw fire, raw fragrance! A true marriage of what was always meant to be one flesh! Mission and prayer! Fire and fragrance!

If this has not piqued your curiosity yet, let the testimony of the Bible and history stir hunger in your heart for what is possible again. We will dive deeper into these topics in the coming chapters, but for starters consider Antioch in Acts chapter 13. A community of prophetic believers, teachers, and many others gave themselves to ministering to the heart of the Lord, prayer, and fasting. Out of this lifestyle of corporate communion, Paul and Barnabas were commissioned on the word of the Holy Spirit to go to the nations. The rest is history! Communion—leading to commissioning and dominion. This was not just a good idea; it was not just the logical next step. It did not come from 10 steps to this, or 20 keys to that, or 72 hours in board meetings. One moment of corporate intimacy interrupted by the voice of the Holy Spirit took their fire and released His fragrance to the world around!

St. Patrick created a similar model—an evangelistic strategy based in day and night singing of the Psalms. A community centered around their individual and corporate lives with Jesus spreading the yeast of the Kingdom to whole villages, cities, and nations. This movement would span many nations and several hundred years! Of course the Moravians have had their impact on human history but also on the modern movements of prayer and missions. Countless churches and organizations have looked to their model of prayer and missions as the key to the first Protestant missions movement.

Where would we be without these past models that carried an element of fullness? We would be weak and hopeless. So today we may be a bit weak, but hopeless we cannot be. Not with the past testimonies of what God has done and is now releasing on a global scale like never before in history! Our strength in the future as the mature warrior Bride will come from our present hope. We are foolish to think that without the hope of what could be that we would ever become what we are not!

Herein lies a key to true and lasting Kingdom building: fire and fragrance! There is much more—many more books, many greater minds, and many great points. But the purpose of this book is to stir desire in its readers for what is possible, what can be, what should be, and what will be. The purpose of this book is to mobilize believers all over the world to believe for and live out the fullness of the Gospel! To begin to come together in authentic community, centered on the presence of Jesus, leading to revival and reformation in the nations.

2

THE PURSUIT OF THE PRESENCE
(SEAN'S STORY)

I n 1982, my parents experienced the greatest pain of their young marriage with the sudden loss of their first son from crib suffocation just ten weeks after his birth. This unfathomable tragedy shook them to the core of their faith and questioned their belief in the goodness of God. Even though they both possessed strong roots in faith-filled families and communities from growing up in the Deep South, this shocking tragedy challenged that entire heritage.

My father had just begun turning the corner on his brand new dermatology practice and my mom was working as a nurse. A call to the unknown led them to "go west, young man" (thanks, Michael W.

Smith) and forge a new practice immediately out of medical school. They gladly exchanged the familiarity, humidity, and hominess of the South for the grandeur, freshness, and beauty of the Montana Rocky Mountains. This pioneering spirit would be caught by every one of their children.

A Child of Promise

New on the scene in the hippie mountain town of Missoula, they were blessed to find their beautiful Assemblies of God church community, which nursed them through the trial of losing their only son. The church people rallied as an agent of healing and released prophetic foresight and encouragement for the season of redemption and promise to come. Shortly after Christopher's death, a word came forth from a rainbow that shined brilliantly across the Missoula Valley and pointed to a sign and promise that redemption and restoration were soon on their way. A year later to the exact day of that heartbreaking loss of 1982, I was born.

Montana is probably the best place in the entire world for an adventurous, mischievous, and free-spirited boy to grow up. The mountains were a perfect getaway for the only boy sandwiched between three sisters (two older, one younger). When I was found guilty of antagonizing or causing harassment to my three sisters, I was banished to remain outdoors for the day.

Our street was near the top of the foothills of the Missoula River Valley. Behind my house was pure unadulterated Rocky Mountain terrain, and it quickly became my playground, my escape, and my joy. Whether sledding through the hills in frigid subzero temperatures or climbing through the woods and across rivers to explore in the summer, my parents only gave me one rule growing up: be at home by 7 P.M. sharp if I wanted dinner. I did not miss a single meal.

Setting the Standard

Things shifted in my family when my parents decided one summer to take a short-term medical mission trip to the war-torn nation of Romania. Little did they know the impact this first mission trip would have or how it would alter the entire course of their family. A heart for the unreached, lost, and sick of the nations began to swell inside my dad. This passion quickly shamed all lesser desires for him to do anything else. After months of wrestling with this God-given mandate heavy on his heart, and while the faces of the lost flooded his dreams, he reached the point of no return. He made the choice to sacrifice his very successful medical practice, which had taken over a dozen years of education to build, for the call of full-time missions to the unreached nations of the world. This one decision established an entirely new value system for my family, and a standard was set of pursuing the call of God at any cost.

God divinely opened a door in 1994 for my parents to work in helping direct and manage an organization called Operation Blessing. This was the justice, mission, and outreach arm of CBN (Christian Broadcasting Network), based in Virginia Beach, Virginia. We relocated from the gorgeous, dry, mountainous, and sparsely populated West to a humid, flat, overcrowded East Coast beach town. It was quite a change, but we embraced it and forged ahead.

During the beginning years in Virginia, my parents led countless trips to unreached nations, raised millions of dollars worth of food, medicine, and resources to distribute overseas, and even outfitted a commercial L1011 airplane to become a literal "flying hospital"! The financial cutbacks and transition from owning a thriving medical practice to full-time ministry began to take a toll. This caused my family to grow closer in that one-year period than during the prior ten years combined! Looking back now, the hand of God was at work as a new identity was being formed and knit for my family.

Once the season with CBN came to a close, yet another shift was on the horizon. My parents felt the voice of God calling us to complete a Crossroads Discipleship Training School as a family together in the city of Kona, Hawaii. Upon hearing the many testimonies from close friends who had completed the course, coupled with the thought of living in Hawaii, the entire family was easily convinced.

I, on the other hand, was the lone soldier who absolutely loathed the idea, and thought it cruel to steal away my prime moments of junior high. Even if it was tropical Hawaii, I had an image I needed to keep up. I was the quarterback of the football team, a captain of the basketball team, and even had a few girls of interest who I thought were interested in me, too. It seemed like a crime to rip this golden life away from a budding teenager saturated in American pop culture! I fought my case very hard, until that day I reluctantly boarded the plane.

The Encounter on the Island

My parents knew what was best for me and did not even think twice about it. Because of their obedience and God's grace over my life, I experienced an encounter with Jesus during the three months in

Hawaii that would mark me for eternity. What was awaiting our family on the beautiful island was three months full of adventure and spiritual download. It was a concentrated dose of seeking God, receiving training and impartation from great teachers from around the world, cramming into the biggest apartment they had on base (still pretty small!), and soaking in the gorgeous sunsets.

Everything in my life changed during that time as I recommitted my heart and life to Jesus in a fresh way and heard the voice of God for the first time. I began to run after God like never before and was filled with the baptism of the Holy Spirit while receiving dreams, visions, and visitations! On top of all this, I learned how to be a decent surfer! My life changed dramatically when I returned to Virginia, as even my close comrades wondered what had changed in my life. I began to plug into my local youth group, started a small group in my house, and took up guitar as my passion for worship grew immensely strong. This encounter in Hawaii sparked the journey that I am still on today. I refer to it simply as "The Pursuit of His Presence."

Raw Beginnings

Upon the return home from Hawaii, I found myself smack-dab in the middle of a genuine move of God exploding in our youth group. My small group quickly grew from 8 to 80 packed into my house. Our youth group exploded from 70 bored kids to 350 rowdy, wild worshiping teens gathering from churches across the city for Wednesday night "Catching Fire." These explosive gatherings were held at a local public primary school that was anything but fancy and slick. We had no cushioned stadium seating, smoke machines, strobe lights, or great pumping sound system. But we did have the unfailing presence of God that showed up every Wednesday and marked us with His glory and encounter. The meetings were raw, honest, authentic, and passionate.

From the time I could strum three chords, I began leading worship. Our entire band sounded horrendous at best. Our drummer was the single bright mark, as he schooled at Berkeley. Needless to say, we thrashed out a few tunes with a few chords and did a whole lot of drum solos! I could never forget how intense those times would get! Often in high moments of intercession and praise, people would spontaneously begin to turn over large trashcans and beat on them with their hands! It was absolutely wild, intense, and free! This was our safe place where we began to learn how to flow with the Holy Spirit through undignified Davidic worship and prophetic song.

Encounter Turned to Outreach

We did not stop with only the encounters. The DNA of "Fire and Fragrance" first took root in my life during these years. We had corporate moments where the fire of His Presence began to burn so hot in us that we just had to release the fragrance to the world around us! We would come directly out of our meetings and pay frequent visits to the local emergency rooms to pray for the sick, depressed, and dying.

Not once did we have anyone refuse prayer for healing and restoration in this place of desperation. We witnessed numerous healings take place and encountered true openness to the Gospel! One summer during our frequent visits, the emergency room literally became emptied of its patients. This prompted the city to even contemplate shutting it down! We also journeyed on evangelistic door-to-door "strikes" on certain neighborhoods, sharing Jesus and praying with whomever would receive it. This yielded incredible testimonies in addition to us being banned by police from many area neighborhoods! One person actually remarked that we were selling Jesus, to which we responded, "But He's a free gift!"

A New Sound

During the height of this move and worship explosion that overtook our community in Virginia, my good friend and mentor at the time, Jason Upton, recorded his first album "Key of David" at one of our gatherings. This was a groundbreaking sound that leaked around the world (thanks to Websites like Napster). It was a catalyst, helping usher in a wave of prophetic, spontaneous, and free worship that we are still experiencing and enjoying today. This took place during this beautiful "open Heaven" season as we stumbled into a realm of powerful encounters with the Holy Spirit. The worshipers, musicians, and leaders from this era are now scattered across the world writing anointed songs, pioneering churches, and serving in the darkest mission frontiers and making Jesus famous across the earth.

Then, There Came a Girl

On this journey of going deeper into the heart of God, there came a girl. Isn't that so timeless and cheesy? Well, it is the truth. This beautiful blue-eyed blonde in my youth group stole my heart. From the first time I laid eyes on her, a voice inside told me that I would be spending the rest of my life with her. I did not bank on some heavy prophetic word from a hyped-up super-spiritual youth leader (thank God!), but I felt the gentle whisper of the Spirit inside of me confirm it.

What made the circumstances more in my favor was that her dad was a youth leader in the same city. I was able to get in good with him before I started pursuing his prized eldest daughter. That was a wise move, and I am still reaping the benefits of it to this day! Kate and I carry the classic high school sweetheart story and truly grew up in God together. That is something I rarely witness today among young married couples, and I am eternally grateful to God for it.

TheCall

The summer before my junior year in 2000, an event took place that changed my life. During this gathering, I was caught up in an open vision that would forever revolutionize my life. Rumors were flying around the East Coast during the summer of a vision of thousands of young people gathering on the Mall in Washington, DC, for an entire day filled with nothing but worship, prayer, and fasting. Without hearing anything more about the event, our fiery crew in Virginia was behind it 100 percent. This was something right up our alley and was already taking place on a smaller local level in our community. We even took up the primary task of mobilizing the entire East Coast for this event named "TheCall."

We phoned hundreds of churches, youth groups, and ministries and held prayer rallies urging everyone to go and contend in the nation's capital. A burned CD began making its way swiftly around our community (thanks again to Napster). "Extreme Disciples" was a sound that stirred our hearts and brought language to what we were all feeling. We also heard that the man with the raspy voice contending and prophesying on the CD was the main leader of this big gathering we were working to mobilize.

We were thoroughly thrilled and knew it would be an assembly of epic proportions no matter who showed up. That September day in 2000, they all came. No one understood how, why, or where they all even came from. Close to a half-million Americans packed out the historic Mall between the Capitol building and the Washington Monument to pray, fast, cry, repent, worship, praise, prophesy, and believe for revival in our land! It was an experience unmatched and truly released supernatural faith into my heart. To walk out on the Mall that day and behold the masses hungry for God caused me to truly believe in this end-time army God is raising up in my generation!

It is one thing to read the epic end-time prophecies in the Book of Joel, but an entirely different reality to witness it become manifest with your very own eyes! The entire day was marked by extreme urgency and intensity as leaders from across denominational, ethnic, and social lines stood together prophetically declaring a season of unity and righteousness across America! What was unfolding in front of me that day was the culmination of many hopes, dreams, prayers, and tears throughout the history of my nation.

The Vision of Fire

I was taken into an open vision during a midday worship session at TheCall, as I was lying prostrate in the grass in the hot afternoon sun. This is one of only three vivid experiences like this in my entire life and would foreshadow my destiny in years to come. During the vision, I was taken up in the heavens and viewed the earth from the vantage point of an astronaut standing on the moon. As I beheld this view, I began to notice little sparks popping up in every continent and virtually every nation of the world.

The sparks grew within a matter of minutes into small flames and replicated over and over again. There were so many of these small flames that the earth was literally filled with a fire that lit up the darkness of the sky and atmosphere. As the flames began to go higher and higher and get brighter and brighter, I heard the audible voice of the Lord speak to me: *"I have called you to light fires across the earth."*

Instantly, I began to see smoke rise from these burning flames and literally canopy the entire earth. There was not an ocean, mountain chain, nation, or continent not completely covered with this thick smoke as it enveloped humanity.

The verse flashed before my eyes from Malachi 1:11:

> *My name will be great among the nations, from the rising to the setting of the sun. In every place, incense and pure offerings will be brought to My name, because My name will be great among the nations...* (Malachi 1:11 NIV).

At that moment, I was filled with vision, life, meaning, and a new drive to see this very thing come to pass on the earth. I did not know how, when, or where—but I knew it was my assignment.

The College Years

Despite my noble idea to finish high school and immediately purchase a one-way ticket to China to sow my life into world missions like

Hudson Taylor, God clearly spoke to me that this was not consistent with His perfect will. Doors flung wide open through scholarships and divine relationships for me to attend Oral Roberts University in the fall of 2002. My aim was to pursue a business degree with a minor in music. I said farewell to my incredible life-giving community, my amazing girlfriend, and the beach as I journeyed across the nation to the flat and hot land of the Midwest. I carried very high hopes and expectations for what was to come. I had heard the many legends and stories of ministries, musicians, and entire movements that were launched out of this small university in Tulsa, Oklahoma, and was ready to become another great story of success. Little did I know that God was leading me into a wilderness season to discover the source of true intimacy leading to authority.

My hopes for success faded away as I spent the entire first year at college doing absolutely no ministry. My heart felt so barren during those first months that I did not even pick up my guitar one time to play. I was not angry or jaded at the church or ministry, but God was beginning to expose a veil of performance, insecurity, and the fear of man residing in my heart. This was the false identity keeping me from going deeper into His heart. It was a lengthy process as God began to root out the unhealthy religious paradigms and expectations I bought into. The big breakthrough began to take place when I finally quit the striving and learned how to lie down and simply rest in His Presence.

The Awakening

Longings began to be awakened during this time in my heart for more of God, and it was not just to write songs, lead large meetings, or be recognized by men. I became hungry to truly know Him deeper!

It is widely known that midnight to 3 A.M. is the most rowdy time in a college dorm—ordering late-night pizza, watching old Seinfeld episodes, playing idiotic pranks, and cramming for exams all take place. But it was during these hours that God began to beckon me away to meet Him in the stairwell on the eighth floor of our dorm tower.

I would dust off my guitar, grab my Bible, and launch into hours of worship, prayer, and face-to-face conversation with God. The reverb created by the sound bouncing off the walls and stairs added to the epic nature of those moments. For nearly the first time in my life, I truly began to experience the reward of being a son of God in His Presence above everything else. He sealed my heart and set me on fire with renewed vision!

Encounter to Movement

As these late-night encounters radically shifted, restored, and reshaped my entire life, my mouth began to be filled with new songs, melodies, and lyrics. I could not help but invite other musicians and worshipers to join into these sessions of glory. I began to cram musicians and worshipers into my small European-sized dorm room to release worship, flow in the spirit, and experience this dynamic presence of God!

These were some of the thickest, most intense and ecstatic experiences of my life! We would sometimes go for hours and hours, and even all night long when it was really good! We were caught up together in realms of glory I cannot even try to articulate with mere words. New songs and sounds were released. Innocence replaced cynicism as the waters of His Presence washed over our hearts and lives. As we met in the evening and released our song, many times we would not end until the following morning.

Word of these encounters quickly spread far and wide! This caused the room to get packed full of people and forced us into finding a larger venue. I began to connect with leaders around the city who burned with a kindred heart of night-and-day worship. Many of us carried a mutual dream of establishing a place free from any other agenda but engaging with and enjoying His Presence. This was initially a foreign concept in a very religious town and our gatherings were first considered to be "rogue" or "without adequate covering" by some city leaders. The opposition to establish this place of unhindered worship was initially so strong that out of over 7,000 churches across the city of Tulsa, we struggled to find a single one that would allow us to use their building.

Freedom for the Psalmist

After much prayer, God provided the perfect location: a place that was completely neutral while embodying our raw zeal. This was a bare and empty storefront conveniently located next to the best coffee joint in town. It carried a similar ambiance as the bare primary school did when our youth group meetings erupted in Virginia. Little did we know how brilliant this strategy was as the delicious artesian lattes fueled the sound of all night worship and prayer! What a glorious and powerful combo!

Musicians, worship leaders, pastors, elders, and college kids from different churches, denominations, and backgrounds began to pack in this little storefront. It felt like a slice of Heaven on earth. It is so ironic that, in a city packed full of megachurches displaying the most innovative and beautiful buildings in Christendom, God would provide a bare, empty, and raw room to birth and ignite this movement. People were drawn to it as something about it set spirits free when they walked in.

A beautiful transition took place as the mantle of the psalmist anointing fell on the worship leaders and musicians of the city. Many once trapped by the spirit of performance were now free to prophesy and release spontaneous songs during these open sessions. Revelation dawned on their hearts that they were not merely meant to carry sing-along song services on Sunday morning, but they were psalmists created to sing the very songs of Heaven carrying breakthrough and life!

Hearts truly came alive in the midnight hours as God called us to be the "watchmen on the walls" over the city as referred to in the Book of Ezekiel (see Ezek. 33:6-7). One of the most amazing testimonies taking place across the city was that this spirit of free and abandoned worship began to spill out through these musicians into their Sunday morning services! The spiritual water level began to rise across the region and it was not restricted to a single church, denomination, or ministry.

We quickly began to increase and expand our worship and prayer hours from 24 to up to 100 hours, and the frequency increased from once per month to bimonthly. The many leaders and pioneers involved in this grassroots movement met together and we all decided that we finally needed a name for what God was doing. We tossed around different ideas but the word that stuck with us all was "The Burn." The decision was made because it was the easiest and simplest word to describe what was taking place during these countless hours in the presence of God. We were asking for the fire of His Presence to come ignite our hearts so we could burn and shine in every area of our life! In a post 9/11 world, we got some serious flack for meddling with terrorist words like "burn." I guess it was a risk worth taking, though, as there was no other way to describe what God was doing in our midst!

A Divine Disturbance

Simultaneously during this time, Kate and I were enjoying the first year of marriage together and had just moved into a new quaint starter home. Things were going financially well for us as the real estate company I started with two other friends from college was beginning to take off. Kate was in school part-time at a local community college and working part-time as well. Our life was peaceful, contained, comfortable, and very convenient. We even had "the burn" as a nice ministry outlet each month as I still continued with minimal travel around the nation leading worship.

The Holy Spirit then came to disrupt our peace and tranquility with frustration and uneasiness! Often, we depict the Person of the Holy Spirit as a Comforter and Counselor, but miss the other aspects of His nature. He does service these roles in our daily lives, but He is not limited to this job description by any means! The Holy Spirit is famous for disrupting and disturbing our lives in order to gain our full attention and align us with the Father's will. We experienced this firsthand during this season.

Originally, I thought it was a demonic stronghold that was bringing me to the edge of insanity! In a matter of a few weeks, I began to feel frustrated, discontent, and irritated at my pretty little life. I had a beautiful wife, a new home, and nothing to complain about. However, I was not happy or fulfilled. I also began to have crazy encounters, dreams, and almost haunting thoughts about the Tabernacle of David and 24/7 worship and prayer.

Now when I say "haunting," I mean just that. These things flooded my thoughts and emotions almost nonstop! I could not get them out of my head. The central verse that consumed me to the core was from Psalm 132:2-5. This was the cry from David's heart:

> *He swore an oath to the Lord and made a vow to the mighty one of Jacob: "I will not enter my house or go to my bed—I will allow no sleep to my eyes or slumber to my eyelids, till I find a place for the Lord, a dwelling for the Mighty One of Jacob"* (Psalm 132:2-5 NIV).

God began to burden my heart with this quest! I began to notice the theme of the Father continually looking for a resting place among His children all throughout the Bible. It reached a tipping point as I could not handle it anymore! This came to a divine culmination late one night as I was praying and waiting on God. In a matter of three days after that night, I quit my business, sold our nice convertible (still miss it), packed up our house, and put a "for sale" sign out front. Kate and I left everything and drove off with our most prized possessions loading down our '98 Toyota Camry.

Risking It All

At this point, I had no clue how bills were going to be paid or if my house would be sold. These and other questions loomed heavy on my heart as we continued on our pursuit. I cannot ever forget how my wife looked at me in that moment we were driving away. With tears rolling down her red cheeks, she softly spoke in a broken voice: "Sean, where are we going and what are we going to do?"

I got pretty choked up as well in that moment and responded by saying: "I have no clue, but we are going to build a place for God to dwell in the nations of the earth."

This is how all this madness began. And here we are three years later: 648,000 air miles, 28 nations, eight full-length albums, thousands of new friends, a full-time school and internship, and 90 burning furnaces of consistent worship, prayer, and missions scattered in cities across the world. God is faithful to fulfill the words He promised! He is dramatically increasing His Presence and it only gets more fun as we continue on this "Pursuit of His Presence" across the nations of the world!

3

A HERITAGE OF REVIVAL
(ANDY'S STORY)

I was born into a small community in the northeastern corner of Washington state. Before my family and their friends had moved there, it had been nothing more than a one-house farm used primarily for logging and disappearing from society. But before I go too far, first let me start a few generations before me. My great-grandmother was a single mom raising five children in difficult times. However, her faith was strong and her trust in a benevolent, faithful God not only gave her the grace to raise her five children, but also filled her with an uncanny desire to know God in a deeper way. This deeper way came to be around the time that the Holy Spirit was being poured out in unprecedented ways in the aftermath of the Azusa Street Revival and the healing revivals of the 1940s and 1950s.

Never to Be the Same

My great-grandmother and her sisters were baptized in the Spirit at a church called Angeles Temple in Southern California. At the time, a radical woman of God named Aimee Semple McPherson was the leader of this church. This season would mark a massive turning point for my family. From this point forward, there has been hunger for revival and reformation coursing through the veins of my family members.

My great uncle (my mom's uncle) was discipled by a man named William Branham. Branham is still considered by many today to have walked in one of the most accurate word of knowledge and healing gifts of anyone documented. Many times he would call out a person's address, phone number, and sickness and then declare healing over them. More often than not, that individual was healed. Many times whole hospital wards were brought to his tent meetings, and often everyone would leave healed! William Branham once said that my uncle was like a son to him. He poured much into him, and it did not go without return! My uncle was involved in the beginnings of the Full Gospel Businessmen, a ministry that God used in the mid-1900s and still continues to use today to go to the nations as well as to fund overseas missions.

Several years ago, I sat around a fireplace with my 89-year-old uncle listening to firsthand stories of himself, William Branham, and Demos Shakarian. These were compelling accounts of miraculous healings, third Heaven experiences, and most of all, radical love for God. He recounted a time he was in Japan and announced that God wanted to heal. Right away, a man with a shriveled arm and hand came up for prayer. As they began to pray, the cracking and popping of bones being formed and muscles being created filled the room as the Holy Spirit began to move in a powerful way. It was soon announced to those attending the meeting at the Pearl Ball Room in the Tokyo Hilton that revival had come to Japan. The man's arm was completely healed. Soon after this, the room was full of reporters and the pastors began to minister deliverance and salvation to those attending.

My uncle went on to tell of a time he was ministering in the nation of Jordan. He was gathered in a church that met on the roof of the pastor's home filled with gun-slinging Arabs curious about the message that was being shared. By the end of the meeting, everyone had given their lives to Jesus. So many had been healed and gone home to get other sick ones that the pastor had to drive a car through the crowd to get my uncle and his co-workers before they were literally crushed.

Another story he related took place during the Full Gospel Businessmen annual offering. As the offering was being taken, several people had given messages in tongues and the interpretations of those messages had followed. My uncle, who was a young man at the time, felt as if his prayer language was a volcanic eruption about to explode. Finally, he could hold it in no longer and began to shout at the top of his lungs a message in a language he could not understand. Because several had already given messages in tongues, one of the older members in the congregation felt that this additional message was out of order. My uncle was publicly rebuked and sat down defeated and discouraged not wanting anything more than to crawl under a nearby rug. As the meeting went further along, they were about to announce the amount of the offering when an attendee asked for permission to speak. The man went on to share that he was the French translator for the United Nations when it was first formed. He said the message my uncle had given was spoken in the highest form of diplomatic French he had ever heard in his life! The translation of the message in tongues was an affirmation of the purpose of the meeting and a prophetic word that more finances than were even needed were going to come in the offering. When the offering was totaled, the word was correct. This was the first time that my uncle realized his prayer language was perfect French.

This zeal for the presence of God and revival was passed to my grandfather, grandma, and mother. At the time, they lived near Los Angeles. One evening in 1970, my grandma convinced my reluctant grandfather to attend a meeting held by a woman named Kathryn Kuhlman. From that point on, they never missed a meeting in Los Angeles and my mother and grandma soon found themselves singing in Kathryn Kuhlman's choir! My grandfather stubbornly refused to sit anywhere but the front row, where he listened intently and recorded each meeting with his lap-size tape recorder. Their stories of healing are as remarkable as any that I have ever heard or read about. Not only of extreme healings, but also of the raw presence of God that would fill the rooms as Mrs. Kuhlman would minister.

A New Beginning

In the late 1970s, my great uncle, grandparents, and mother moved up to a sleepy little valley in northeast Washington to build a Christian community that would escape the dilapidation of American morals and values. They started over, building each others' homes, sharing everything, including the community cow, and meeting regularly to just worship, fellowship, and learn from my uncle the principles and values of the Kingdom. It was into this environment and heritage that I was born in June 1980. I was born into an atmosphere that would naturally lend itself to a hunger for revival and the Presence of God. The supernatural was normal; the Bible was the absolute standard for all of life; we lived in authentic community; and His Presence inhabiting the earth was the ultimate goal.

We left this community in 1988, as many of the young couples who had moved there were now married and had children, and the lack of finances coming into the community from the scarce jobs forced many of the families to move back into civilization to find work. This pilgrimage landed my family of four into the only place I could have imagined more remote than our Washington hideaway: the Aleutian Islands in the great state of Alaska!

My dad had been stationed on an island named Adak during the Vietnam War and had fallen in love with the remote, barren, wind-blown island. It was famous for its 100-mile-per-hour winds and lack of any trees. The next ten years of my life would be spent in Alaska. Four of those years were on the island of Adak and six in the beautiful little town of Homer. Just as memories of my childhood faded over time, so did my sense of the Lord's nearness and power. Most of my junior high and high school years were spent in the ups and downs of apathetic Christianity.

But God was not done with my family or me. The relentless Hound of Heaven finally caught up with me, shortly after I graduated high school. I naively committed six months to doing a Discipleship Training School with Youth With a Mission in Maui, Hawaii. What Alaskan wouldn't want to spend a winter in Maui? Little did I know the fire that God would re-stoke in my heart during this time. I am forever indebted to YWAM for reintroducing to me the intimate Savior of the lost, the loving Father of all creation, and the life-changing power of the Holy Spirit. It was through YWAM that God gripped my heart for the nations of the earth. I began to carry a burning desire in my own heart to see a marriage between seeking the presence of God and living a life prioritizing and releasing that presence as the strategy for reaching every nation on earth.

Stones of Remembrance

I remember key moments along the journey when I felt the Lord drop revelation into my heart to continue me on a path of pursuing this dream. I remember sitting for hours in a little room in the basement of our old kitchen in Maui after having read *Red Moon Rising* by Pete Grieg and dreaming what would be possible if the Bride of Christ became "hot" in the presence of God and really took that fire to the streets. I remember an extended fast that felt much more like a feast as I daily asked God to raise up His worshipers and intercessors around the earth from every tribe and tongue. I remember flying into Hong Kong one evening in 2004 and gazing at the beautiful cityscape and feeling the Lord whisper in my ear, "Houses of prayer and worship in every nation of the earth."

I recall standing on a rooftop in Kathmandu, Nepal, gazing at the distant Himalayas and pondering the recent collapse of the Nepali monarchy. Because of the people crying out against the monarchy and basically forcing a new form of government, they had undermined the entire Hindu system that is based on an idea that the king is a reincarnation of one of the primary Hindu gods. If they have no king, in essence, they have no reincarnation of their god. As I watched the deep, red sun setting against the beautiful cityscape I was in awe of what the Lord was doing in this war-torn nation. As clear as the approaching night sky, the Lord reminded me that there had been a faithful remnant of Nepalis who were rescued from the streets and rescued from

Hinduism. They had been praying day and night for over eight years that the Kingdom of God would break in.

I remember waking up in the middle of the night in Kona, Hawaii, to a voice saying over me, "This thing is like a disease that is difficult to catch, but when you do, it will completely consume you." I knew this thing to be a movement of hunger for God that will soon grip the entire earth like a disease that is incurable. It may not come easy, but when it does, it consumes!

A Divine Appointment for All Time

Years ago, I was at a church and ministry called MorningStar in Fort Mill, South Carolina. A man whom I did not know and have never seen again prophesied that something of God was going to come out of Dallas, Texas. He stressed that I was meant to connect with it. This is where my and Sean's stories beautifully collide. I was in Maui teaching for a week at the YWAM school. It just so happened that during the same week, some friends from the previous years of being involved with YWAM Maui were getting married. It also divinely happened that Sean had grown up going to high school with the bride. This would prove to be the most anointed bachelor party I have ever been to!

I don't remember anything else from the bachelor party except a three-hour conversation with Sean where the Lord began to instantly knit our hearts and histories together. We began to realize that we both possessed the same passion for the presence of God exalted and enjoyed in the place of worship and prayer, as well as to see this foundation of ministry explode into the darkest and hardest of places.

It wasn't until over a year later, as we met up in different states and countries, that it dawned on me that Sean was from Dallas and that this movement of Burn 24-7 was exactly what the Lord was talking about six years prior!

This story represents two in the midst of thousands and thousands of others who are coming together all over the world with a passion for the fiery presence of God, heart-rending revival, and society-shifting reformation. The DNA of these communities is organically forming all over the world. We are truly on the verge of a grassroots righteousness movement that is going to sweep the earth like a windblown forest fire! Authentic community centered around the raw presence of God that inevitably leads to revival and reformation!

The Beacons Are Lit

Perhaps these two stories and the vision emerging can best be summarized through the following scene of a familiar movie.

I was in the middle of an extended fast and one night I found myself sitting in my bed watching *The Lord of the Rings* on a premonition from the Lord that He had a specific message for me to behold. Night after night, I watched half-hour increments waiting for something to jump out. Finally, hours into the extended versions, I sat in awe as I watched a scene unfold that would mark me forever.

An unlikely hobbit valiantly climbed a tower with nothing but dry wood at the top. As he tipped a container of oil and dropped a burning torch, soon the whole stack of wood was in massive flames!

A process began that could not be stopped. What unfolds next is a scene of epic proportions as the camera pans across massive mountain ranges, through the day and through the night as one towering beacon after another is lit by little-known but heroic figures. Their eyes had been trained and hearts had been prepared for the chain reaction that would bring them into their destinies. As the fires went from mountaintop to mountaintop, they ended in a community of humans who realized the fire was a cry for help from another community that was soon to be attacked. A man drinking his morning coffee was the first to see the last beacon burn and he quickly mobilized an army to rush to the aid of the other community.

I stared in amazement as the Lord spoke to me that the beacons represented a people filled with zeal for the presence of God. The beacons were lit by the faithful, yet relatively unknown heroes of a watchful generation. The man who had seen the last beacon was in fact the rightful king, and the event that ensued was nothing less than the title of the movie: *The Return of the King*.

As I write this I am sitting in my hotel room in Hong Kong. Tomorrow, over 1,000 Chinese believers will be gathering together with others from over 100 countries to commune with God and each other to discuss the completion of a 2,000-year assignment to see every tribe, tongue, and nation hear the Gospel. I am convinced that the beacons are rapidly being lit!

They will not be stopped. Communities of both earthly obscurity and heavenly royalty are assembling all over the world. The oil of intimacy is being poured out all over the earth as God calls His beloved Bride back to His side. The fire of desire is burning brighter and brighter. Prayer is going up all over the world like never before in history. Miracles are breaking out in unprecedented fashion. Though darkness will make its best effort, nothing will stop these fires from burning across the earth, and eventually the King himself will see the fire He first came to kindle. The fire He has longed to see! He will rise up as a Mighty Warrior with fire in His eyes, and the Return of the King will go from movie title to reality!

4

HEAVEN'S PERSPECTIVE

The word *perspective*, though used much, is little understood and way too infrequently put into practice for a redemptive purpose! Everyone has a perspective. It is not a matter of having it or not. The question is who is dictating our perspective, what determines our perspective, and what values are shaping our perspective.

Just think for a moment. This morning you woke up and you began to view your day and your life with a specific perspective. That perspective will determine the tint with which you view all of life. It will either release life or death, joy or depression, risk or fear. I believe this to be one of the greatest battles for Christians in this day. How will we choose to view life, hardship, potential, and our purpose as believers on this earth?

For way too many, the primary shaper of our perspectives on life is our circumstances. We have become slaves to our circumstances and live most of our life responding to what may come. These responses are not all negative, but result in a life of defensive move after defensive move rather than a continual move forward as a disciplined army taking battlefield after battlefield on a road to sure victory! For many of us, we take in our perspectives from the recent headlines written from a primarily negative, ungodly, and extremely humanistic news media. If this becomes our daily food and report card on the well-being or advancement of the Kingdom, then it is no wonder why the Body struggles with a sense of hope for the future. Often, this only feeds our propensity toward cynicism and skepticism rather than stirring faith for the seemingly impossible.

An Overcoming Perspective

Where are the Davids in our generation who will look at the giants in the land and view them through the lens of an unstoppable Kingdom? This is a Kingdom that knows no permanent defeat, but only temporary setbacks, and always has the potential for the kiss of redemption. David looked at the giant, Goliath, with nothing but indignation that this man would mock the living God. He carried total confidence that he was not going to allow this to continue. It is time that the members of the Body of Christ begin to wake up in the morning, strap on our swords, put on the mind of Christ, and walk through our day with the anticipation of one giant after another falling! It is time that we stop dwelling on our circumstances—no matter how difficult or how bleak they may seem—and laugh at the enemy's pathetic attempts to stop the spread of an unstoppable Kingdom! With this perspective, who can stop us?

Many times we forget that Jesus calls us the "the light of the world." We often think of Jesus as the Light of the world, and He certainly is, as He declares in John 8:12. But He does not stop there. In Matthew 5:14, Jesus declares boldly that, *"You are the light of the world. A city that is set on a hill cannot be hidden."* Have you ever flipped a light switch in a room and before your eyes watched a battle take place as the light emanating from the lightbulb works to overcome the darkness in the room? Have you ever seen darkness hold its ground over the light of a candle or the dawn's first rays? In the same manner, we cannot lose this battle! No headline, no government, no weakness of man, no army of hell, and no economic collapse can stop the spread of the light of the Kingdom in our day!

Imagine what life would be like if every believer in the world woke up in the morning and the first thought was of the victory of Christ on the cross, the life He died to give us, the power of the Holy Spirit now living within each one of us, and the strength of our Daddy above every other daddy in the world! This army of believers would have the ability to bring massive change and transformation all over the world. They would truly be the manifestation of light breaking into every nation, every sphere, and every heart!

Take the Land

Consider the Scriptures on this matter of the Kingdom breaking in and His glory being released. Allow the authoritative, perfect Word of God to release fresh perspective of not only what is possible but of what is non-negotiable and inevitable. In Numbers 13:2, the 12 spies are sent into the land of Canaan to *"spy out the land of Canaan, which I am giving to the children of Israel..."* Take note that

God did not send them into the land to evaluate their ability to overcome the inhabitants of the land. But He commanded them to simply "spy out" the land that "I am giving to you." This was a non-negotiable in the heart of the Lord. Yet 10 of the 12 still went into the land evaluating their ability to take the land through the lens of human possibility rather than the lens of the sure, never-failing promise of God. Naturally, the giant people and their walled cities were too overwhelming for the spies' small-minded perspectives. The end result was death, wandering, and the delayed fulfillment of the promises of God. Only 2 of the 12 were able to see their circumstances in the light of the glory of the eternal God. Their response to the cynical 10 was, *"Only do not rebel against the Lord, nor fear the people of the land, for they are our bread; their protection has departed from them, and the Lord is with us…"* (Num. 14:9). In other words, we will eat these guys for lunch because God made us a promise and He knows how to keep it!

How often do we live our lives like the ten, continually evaluating what we consider to be possible or what we feel we are capable of? Besides, when was it about human capability or circumstantial possibilities anyways? No hero has ever become a hero by walking according to the possible. No Joshua has ever taken the land by evaluating his own abilities, and no David has ever defeated the giant by the strength of his own sword! If God be for us, who can be against us? It was this decision to live by self-evaluation and analysis that caused a paralysis of faith and kept these men and this massive army from their promised birthright. However, it is also on the heels of this decision that God used the opportunity to make a promise that will release ridiculous, life-giving confidence into every one of our own hearts, lives, and circumstances: *"But truly, as I live, all the earth shall be filled with the glory of the Lord"* (Num. 14:21).

In other words, unless you can kill God, nothing will stop the release of His glory over the whole of the earth! What a promise! What a declaration! What if these statements from God became our primary food for thought?

Solomon's Petition

Apparently, this was the case for Solomon, who 500 years later seemed to make this promise the fuel for his petition in Psalm 72:18-19.

> *Blessed be the Lord God, the God of Israel, who only does wondrous things! And blessed be His glorious name forever! And let the whole earth be filled with His glory. Amen and Amen* (Psalm 72:18-19).

Solomon grabbed onto the promise of God for his life and released this petition of agreement, in essence saying, *"Lord, let it be in my day and in my life!"* Solomon's faith for agreement and petition rests firmly on the shoulders of the promise God made 500 years previous in Numbers 14. Imagine Solomon as he reflected on the faithfulness of God to fulfill this promise to a group of onetime slave laborers, then desert nomads, and now a mighty army with peace on all borders and wealth beyond any other nation! They possessed so much wealth and favor now that even the queen of Sheba made a trip just to see if the reports were true! Solomon's agreement with the release of God's glory was based on the confidence of the promise of God. Where is this confidence today? Do we have any reason to doubt God and His faithfulness to His promises?

Heaven's Perspective

If this is not enough, consider Isaiah 6, written 200 years after this petition in the heart of Solomon and 700 years after the promise of God Himself.

> *In the year that King Uzziah died, I saw the Lord sitting on a throne, high and lifted up, and the train of His robe filled the temple. Above it stood seraphim; each one had six wings: with two he covered his face, with two he covered his feet, and with two he flew. And one cried to another and said: "Holy, holy, holy is the Lord of hosts; the whole earth is full of His Glory"* (Isaiah 6:1-3).

So not only do we have the promise of God and the petition of Solomon, but now the perspective of Heaven! As the inhabitants of Heaven look down on the earth from the throne room of God, they can't help but declare the holiness of the God of the armies of Heaven! Their perspective of our planet in the context of their surroundings is, "The whole earth is full of His glory." In their eyes, His glory is already covering the earth and all that separates us from seeing this is a thin veil of unbelief, the weight of sin, and our human, earthly perspectives. Once again, heroes are made when they can lift the temporary veil of earthly perspective and peer through the eyes of Heaven on the glory of God that even now covers the earth! Then they will be able to call this glory forth like lava from the depths! These moments are what we call revival, a miracle, or the Kingdom breaking in! Oh, to live constantly in this reality of Heaven!

One day last year, I was feeling a bit overwhelmed by some difficult circumstances going on. I was pressing in for a breakthrough in some specific areas that had not yet come. As I began to ask the Lord about this breakthrough and express my concern that it may never come, I sensed the Lord ask me a question: "Andy, do you think the angels are ever insecure about the outcomes?" This question set me back a bit as I really began to ponder the ridiculousness of my own fear and insecurity in God's ability to release His Kingdom on His earth. A second question then came: "Do you think the angels are ever insecure in My leadership?"

Just think for a moment with me: Thunder, lightning, and creatures with eyes, wings, and eyes on their wings. Millions of angels, a floor made of glass, rainbows made up of colors with no names, and the noise of millions singing. Most of all, think of the Lord Himself, high and lifted up, seated on a throne, full of unapproachable light! Now imagine these angels as they look down on the wee little earth. As they gaze down, they see injustice, financial difficulty, relational brokenness, marriages that need healing, the lost who need salvation, addictions that need breaking, and lots of other truly difficult circumstances. Now imagine the emotion running through the hearts of these angels. Do you think that insecurity in God's ability to step into these situations and bring breakthrough ever occurs to them? Do you think they ever feel insecure in the leadership of God? Do they ever question the validity of His promises or the potential of His Kingdom overcoming? Their perspective leads to their confidence and expectation.

Imagine if we lived with the continual confidence of Heaven. We were always intended to live and think within this perspective. To feel the breath of God on our necks and the wind of Heaven on our backs as we march forward with the spiritual, not physical, violence of an overcoming Kingdom! Insecurity does not exist in the perspective of Heaven. So why should it exist on earth? If Heaven lives in a continual state of divine optimism, why should we live any differently?

Habakkuk's Prophecy

So not only is the release of the glory of God a promise He makes on His own life, the petition of King Solomon, and the perspective of Heaven, but Habakkuk makes it a point of nonnegotiable prophecy when he declares in 2:14: *"For the earth will be filled with the knowledge of the glory of the Lord, as the waters cover the sea."* There should not be any doubt in our minds of what the Lord intends to accomplish on this earth.

Perspective. The issue is not what is God doing or going to do; the issue is are we going to see it, agree with it, and be part of bringing it? This is the stuff that creates heroes. What will wake you up and become your food for thought, your foundation for emotion, and your confidence for what is possible? Will we continue to be a people who deconstruct, criticize, and dwell on what is wrong? Or will we become a people who believe in the promise, join with the petition, see with the perspective, and fulfill the prophecy that God's glory is already and will continue to cover the earth? Kingdom now, Kingdom coming, Kingdom here!

Each of us has the choice. David had the choice. His brothers and the majority of the army of Israel were only viewing the circumstances in the light of what they felt was possible. They had truly entered into an unhealthy analysis that had resulted in the paralysis of fear and unbelief. An unlikely shepherd boy stepped into the exact same setting with even less going for him than the older, more experienced soldiers and yet he carried one thing that not one of them had: perspective! Could this be our mightiest weapon?

> *"Your servant has killed both lion and bear; and this*
> *uncircumcised Philistine will be like one of them, seeing*

he has defiled the armies of the living God." Moreover David said, "The Lord, who delivered me from the paw of the lion and from the paw of the bear, He will deliver me from the hand of this Philistine…" (1 Samuel 17:36-37).

The Lord who promised the release of His glory in Numbers 14 will surely deliver on His Word! The God who conquered death on the cross will never be overcome!

Then David said to the Philistine, "You come to me with a sword, with a spear, and with a javelin. But I come to you in the name of the Lord of hosts, the God of the armies of Israel, whom you have defiled" (1 Samuel 17:45).

The world comes with its arsenal of weapons, but we come with the armor of perspective, built on the testimony of our God's faithfulness.

This day the Lord will deliver you into my hand, and I will strike you and take your head from you. And this day I will give the carcasses of the camp of the Philistines to the birds of the air and the wild beasts of the earth, that all the earth may know that there is a God in Israel. Then all this assembly shall know that the Lord does not save with sword and spear; for the battle is the Lord's, and He will give you into our hands (1 Samuel 17:46-47).

Then we shall know that this victory and the release of this glory is not up for debate. We have not been sent to evaluate our ability to walk in victory and release His Kingdom. He has overcome the world, and this is the lens that we choose to view all of life from!

This is the perspective that can birth revival in the face of any circumstances and any society at any depth of depravity. This is the perspective that can step into any workplace, sphere of society, or nation and bring the light of Christ. This is the perspective that can stare an issue like abortion in the face and believe for reformation. Revival and reformation will not be possible without a perspective of a victorious Kingdom and an earth that is now filled and will continue to be filled with the knowledge of the glory of God! Only with this mind-set can we live with hope, and only with hope can we lead the Bride into her greatest hour, her hour of fullness!

5

RESTORING DAVID'S TENT

God is restoring the spirit of worship in our day at a rate none of us can possibly fathom! At the very moment you are reading these words, burning hearts are gathered in prayer rooms, churches, street corners, pubs, coffee shops, under bridges, and in the most random places imaginable pouring out their hearts and love to the one true God. Because 95 percent of the global population lives outside the boundaries of North America and the fastest-growing church in the world resides in Asia, most of these worshiping warriors are not Caucasian and speak a language other than English. Isn't that a refreshingly beautiful thought?

The nations are now worshiping on a level never seen in the history of the world. This movement of first love is exploding faster and farther than at any time in history. Songs, sounds, melodies, rhythms, frequencies, decrees, and prayers are all mingling and colliding together in unified expression and flooding the atmosphere over cities, regions, and communities with the fragrance of Heaven! The prophecy in Malachi 1:11 is coming to pass:

> *"My name will be great among the nations, from the rising to the setting of the sun. In every place incense and pure offerings will be brought to My name, because My name will be great among the nations,"* says the Lord Almighty (Malachi 1:11 NIV).

It is an aroma carrying faith, healing, hope, and life to all who hear it. It is not just cute, orderly church songs in perfect sequence and pitch but a wild, spontaneous, prophetic roar of violent love and affection carrying new authority, fresh passion, and authentic zeal!

The Tabernacle of David was a physical place in the Old Testament located in the City of David, and it was an earthly forerunner to this movement of night-and-day worship sprouting up all over the earth in our day. From this tabernacle, King David organized, mobilized, and facilitated unending night-and-day worship that lasted 33 years! This was no small feat and easily the largest project of David's tenure as leader over the nation of Israel. He personally employed over 4,000 Levitical musicians, singers, scribes, and psalmists in priestly duty for the job of manning night-and-day worship, praise, and proclamation.

Every musician David employed for the tabernacle was a skilled artisan who carved and created his own instrument. They were also required to be proficient enough on their instrument to play anything at any time and to memorize the entire Torah (Old Testament) word perfect. The active musicians were under mentorship from older and more seasoned psalmists until they themselves became mentors after their term of ministering had ended. This was the first and only tabernacle in Israel's long history that did not require any kind of blood sacrifice. The lone offering necessary was the sacrifice of worship, praise, and adoration. It was also the only tabernacle in the Old Testament that was accessible to all worshipers regardless of family, tribe, or social status. David's Tabernacle displayed and prophesied a day of accessibility that would soon come upon the earth where every nation, tribe, and tongue could gain access to the presence of God through the shed blood of Jesus Christ.

A Climate of Creativity, Spontaneity, and Prophecy

Many of the songs recorded in the Book of Psalms were birthed from this place of unending night-and-day worship. It was the artistic epicenter of fresh creativity for the culture of that day. New sounds, moving rhythms, striking melodies, and robust lyrics of adoration, intercession, and praise were flowing forth every second of every day! Imagine a steady and constant stream of revelation, depth of sound, and richness of lyrics that did not stop for over 33 years. This had to have been a place that attracted the nearness of God.

This worship expression King David established relied heavily on prophetic and spontaneous revelation to guide the flow of songs and prayers. Beautiful artistic surprises were around every corner. Musicians, psalmists, and worshipers were encouraged to go "off the page" and be caught up in a greater realm of glory. This is why we observe the command "sing a new song" reiterated over 80 times throughout the Book of Psalms. Every new revelation of the character and person of God demands a new expression through sound and worship. Moments like these take place all over Psalms, as the climate of the nearness of God established through the vertical worship would birth prophetic unction.

In this atmosphere, even David released prophetic songs that foretold major coming events in the history of the world. One of the many examples of this is captured in Psalm 22. During this spontaneous song, David sings the very words the Son of Man would later broadcast on the cross at Calvary over 1,500 years later. What a prophetic zone they were caught up in! Can you imagine being in a worship service where a singer sings with accuracy about events taking place thousands of years in the future? This clearly depicts an atmosphere that was pregnant with revelation and conducive to steward fresh downloads from Heaven while faithful musicians keep this fire on the altar burning.

The Promise of the Presence

During this season of unending worship lasting 33 years, David's kingdom grew in wealth and stature as peace surrounded him on every side. I believe the ultimate purpose of David's Tabernacle was to prophetically foreshadow the man Jesus Christ, who would walk the earth many generations later and the freedom of God's presence that would be released to mankind. Not only did the day and night worship last the exact amount of Jesus' life on earth, but it depicted a day where blood sacrifices were no longer adequate. The sacrifice of praise would be the sound to usher in the presence of God now accessible to all mankind.

We are living in the day of the restoration of David's fallen tent, according to Amos 9:11 and Acts 15:16: *"In that day I will restore David's fallen tent. I will repair its broken places, restore its ruins, and build it as it used to be"* (NIV).

This restoration of David's tent is an invitation to every people group, culture, and nation to enter into the promise of His Presence. Salvation is here, and Jew or Gentile are now welcome to "taste and see that He is good" according to Psalm 34:8 and invite the person of God to make permanent residence inside their hearts. This is the most important of the many promises afforded us to be the fulfillment of this prophetic word.

Literal Fulfillment

Another aspect of this prophetic promise is the literal rebuilding of night-and-day creative, fiery, and vertical worship that is rapidly taking place all over the earth. Thousands of furnaces, boiler rooms, prayer rooms, and all-night worship services are popping up all over the planet! So many in fact, that it is impossible to even put a number on them! Musicians, artists, psalmists, intercessors, and lovers of God from virtually every nation on earth are once again rebuilding the altar of unending adoration, love, and passionate release to God. A definite shift is already underway as we see evident in the perpetual gatherings of the masses as they are coming to worship, pray, and simply be in His Presence. The rebuilding has begun, the restoration is here, and the Kingdom is at hand.

Whether it is in the underground church caves in China, the Himalayan mountain cliffs of Nepal, the slums within the trash heaps in

Burundi, or the state-of-the-art contemporary buildings of Scandinavia, the prophetic song of the Lord is coming forth! Leaders, pastors, and apostolic fathers and mothers are exchanging their slick church agendas for the freedom and simplicity of getting lost in the beauty of His Presence. The Church is beginning to wholly embrace our true identity as "people of His Presence." Revelation is dawning on the global Body that we are indeed fashioned, formed, and created to take our place in the night-and-day worship activities of Heaven! We will be gathered before the throne of God for all of eternity shouting at the top of our lungs "Holy, Holy, Holy" according to the mere glimpse of this we see in Revelation 4. This shift is well underway across the Church worldwide and is resulting in an increased manifestation of His glory in our midst.

Return to the First Love

Possibly one of the most beautiful aspects of this Davidic restoration encompassing the earth is the call for the Bride to return to her first love. At times I believe that we have become so crafty with our knowledge, programs, resources, and methods in the Western church that it has become easy to forget and silence the cry of first love burning deep in our hearts. In many ways, we have built a model and machine of church that can actually run quite smoothly while neglecting the cost of cultivating true intimacy with the Father and receiving the favor, grace, and power that can only be given from this place.

A few months ago, I was gathered with our Burn 24-7 leadership from across the world at our annual global summit in Dallas. Leaders had flown in from continents all over the world for a time of building relationship, seeking God together for strategy, and the best barbecue to ever touch our mouths! The topic of one of our intense conversations—or "skull sessions" as I call them—was bringing definition to the call of Burn 24-7 in one simple sentence. Now we have paragraphs, pages, and bullet points on pamphlets, Websites, and videos describing the many visions, passions, and mandates we are involved with around the world. These include global missions, social justice, feeding programs, schools, internships, recording projects, and so much more.

As I (Sean) was working to put all these on paper in one ridiculously long, massive, run-on sentence, the Spirit whispered in my ear *"Did you already forget? It is all about coming back to the first love."* Instantly, memories flooded my mind of the way too many bodies packed in my little dorm room worshiping their guts out with reckless abandonment. The sound of it all echoed in my ears and reverberated in my soul. Conviction fell heavy upon my heart and my face hit the ground that day.

This rebuilding of David's tent is the return to the hillside where the true commissioning takes place. In this season of expansion and Kingdom dominion across the earth, we cannot be a people or a church that forsakes the first love as was spoken against the church of Ephesus in Revelation 2. Nor can we have any hope to accomplish the second greatest commandment of outreach and missions if we are lousy at and purposefully neglect the first. The first commandment always empowers the second commandment. Busyness is not an excuse. Ministry is not an excuse. Evangelism is not an excuse. Family is not even an excuse. We do not have hope at adequately sharing love with our spouses, children, parents, or neighbors without first going to the Source of true love. The move of worship and prayer being ushered to the earth allows us the opportunity to accurately reprioritize our lives and return back to the first love.

The Place of Encounter

We are consistently surprised and amazed to see what takes place when we heed the cry of Jesus in the opening chapter of the Book of Acts. He pleads with the early church to wait or "tarry" in Jerusalem until the impartation of fire is released. Imagine that! They had just served with Him for many months and years. They had traveled together far and wide, watched Him perform the greatest miracles the earth had ever seen, heard all His sermons and teachings, and even received His rebukes. And at this point, they had even begun to preach, teach, and perform miracles, and do it all themselves!

They must have been overjoyed to share the news from their burning hearts of what had just happened through the resurrection of the Man they loved! They were never more eager or prepared to do this in their entire lives than right then. So what does Jesus tell them to do? Wait for the encounter. Why would He say such a thing? There was a measure of breakthrough that Jesus wanted to see released on their lives that could not be taught, learned, or even gleaned from prior experiences. It came in the form of the Holy Spirit and it had to be caught in the place of encounter.

People often ask me in cities across the world: Can you teach us about this "burn thing," give the mechanics for how it all works, and tell our musicians and worshipers how to be free in the presence of God? At first, I worked hard to break down every explanation, biblical precedent, and function of this movement of rebuilding David's tent in order to help people understand. While all that is good and necessary at times, what I finally realized is that there is nothing that can substitute the experience in His Presence and truly "catching" it for themselves. There is a revelation that is caught more than it ever is taught. Every human being is created to join in this song, and when we gather in the presence of God around the throne, it becomes so naturally supernatural to simply burn before Him with this expression of worship!

Seasonal Shift

One of my great heroes of the faith, and a true mother and pioneer to the movement of burning hearts arising across the world, is Heidi Baker. Heidi prophesied a word over me and my team of 12 musicians, worshipers, and revivalists when we were leaving for a two-month-long Burn 24-7 tour across Europe. The word came out of Song of Songs 2 and focused on the seasonal shift that is currently taking place across the globe. It is a "season of singing" where the "winter has passed and the springtime has come" (see Song of Sol. 2:11-12). We are truly headed into a new day where fragrance of the knowledge of Jesus will flood the earth! We must understand the total fulfillment of the Tabernacle of David does not only come reinstituting the sound of night-and-day worship alone. But there is a divine shift making way for a new season to come upon humanity. This is revealed in the verses that directly follow the call to rebuild the tabernacle in Amos 9:13:

> *"The days are coming," declares the Lord, "when the reaper will be overtaken by the plowman and the planter by the one treading grapes. New wine will drip from the mountains and flow from all the hills"* (Amos 9:13 NIV).

This verse prophesies this shift already taking place across the earth in response to the restoration of the sound of worship and prayer. From the place of encounter in these furnaces, we will then be commissioned to bring healing to a dying world. The legendary release of fire and glory from the Acts 2 upper room experience marked the first encounter with the Holy Spirit by the early church. It also ignited the first major missions, justice, and outreach movement the world had ever seen. That single encounter was the birthplace of a new sound that ushered in a new wave of passionate preaching of the Word with boldness, supernatural signs and wonders, and authentic, sustaining salvation. This all led to the complete transformation of the culture of the day.

We are beginning to experience the fullness of what we have been promised as the Spirit is taking over complete control of our humble prayer rooms, worship services, and furnaces. From the place of stoking the flame of first love, we are hearing the true heartbeat of the Father, and He is commissioning us to spread the fire across the earth! Our songs, prayers, and petitioning are beginning to manifest the authentic fruit of salvation on the earth. This sound arising from the passionate grassroots army across the nations of the earth is the mighty throng from every nation, tribe, and tongue belting out the chorus from Revelation 22:17: *"The Spirit and the bride say, 'Come!'"*

Throne Room Worship

What a beautiful day we are living in as the sound of this "throne room worship" is being established across the nations of the world. This is not restricted to simply Burn 24-7 furnaces, houses of prayer, great conference events, or any particular denomination, but it is a move that is all encompassing and sweeping the planet! Our ears are shutting out the pessimistic and humanistic noises from society and we are tuning in to hear and heed the call from Song of Solomon 2 to "come away" to the deeper and higher places in His Presence.

We are even losing the long-standing predictability of our services and allowing the Holy Spirit to lead us on a journey into the heart of God. Three fast songs followed by three slow songs is no longer the norm as we follow a River full of surprises and adventure! No longer are services and ministries being driven alone by the charismatic personalities of gifted ministers, but by the atmosphere of intense worship and hunger resting on many of these meetings—it is placing a demand on Heaven. This demand is causing Heaven to respond and release the good gifts that have been promised to the children of God. Extraordinary miracles, genuine salvations, astonishing healings, open visions, dreams, and encounters are becoming commonplace. A raw sound of desire is bringing in the lost, hurting, and hungry as it's an authentic cry pulling them in deeper.

A transition is in effect and shifting the landscape of the global Church. What a timely and gorgeous transition it is! Once, we used to gather and flock around the pulpit to hear and receive from gifted and anointed ministers, teachers, and prophets. Our primary goal was to receive while worship was often used to "warm us up" or "prepare our hearts" for the minister to move. While this is not altogether a wrong motivation, it simply represents a former and lesser pattern of thinking.

A new day is dawning on the Church as we are on a journey from "glory to glory" according to Second Corinthians 3:18. Our hearts are swelling and blazing for Him alone! The activities of Heaven are now becoming the activities of earth as we corporately gather around the throne of God as witnessed in Revelation 4. Our sole purpose and number one priority is worshiping Him in Spirit and in truth. New spontaneous songs, frequencies of faith, and rhythms of love are being loosed as a mighty wave of fresh creativity and freedom crashes on the people of God. Our focus and attention is shifting from receiving from "the man of God" to pouring out adoration, love, and worship on the "Person of God" dwelling in our midst.

The Renaissance Has Begun

Along with this explosion of throne room worship currently catching fire all over the earth, we are going to see the Church begin to shine more brightly through music and the arts than ever before. As our schedules, formulas, and agendas are shattered and rearranged by the radiating glory of His raw presence dwelling in our midst, a new freedom and drive is being released on the musicians, artists, poets, and songwriters. The well of creativity is beginning to be uncapped as we connect directly with the Creator of the Universe who continues to reveal new facets of His person each time we come before Him.

These new facets are compelling us to express the majesty of who He is in new ways. Songs, melodies, poems, painting, and dance are coming forth from another realm that all points back to display Him. As this environment of throne room worship is cultivated in our midst, I believe we are going to begin to see the most radical renaissance of the arts that the Church has ever witnessed in history. This has already taken place to some degree, but I believe it is only the very beginning.

I see a day where the Church is once again leading the way in the arena of arts and music around the world. Car stereos, televisions, movie screens, and homes will soon be flooded with the beautiful, intricate, and creative sound of throne room worship that beckons even the lost in deeper. Books will be filled with vibrant poetic imagery describing the stunning encounters in His Presence and colors, feelings, and expressions that have not been captured before. The world will then begin to wonder where such depth of inspiration and new creativity could come from.

It Is the Hour

This is the most exciting and thrilling time in history as we witness the nations of the world build altars of night-and-day worship and prayer. This act is the only response to His goodness and faithfulness. We know that when we call on His name and pursue after His Presence, He will flood and invade our communities, cities, and nations. The dramatic surge in this worship and prayer movement is astounding. It is exploding at such a rapid pace that it is impossible to gather the most current data or even configure the scope of the move.

Only just 30 years ago, there were only a handful of prayer furnaces, houses of prayer, or places of continual worship on the earth. The example throughout history of the Moravians and Celts was all but forgotten. There was not a significant or widespread move of 24/7 worship and prayer that was largely known around the world. The restoration of the Tabernacle of David was being taught by a few pioneers but not considered a high priority in most churches or ministries.

The Modern Forerunners and Pioneers

Despite this seeming waywardness, God always delivers the timely answer. He raised up forerunners, pioneers, and champions who carried a Davidic heart to see sustained prayer and worship become a mainstay in the Church once again. Men and women like Joy Dawson, a teacher from the bustling Youth With a Mission (YWAM) movement, traveled the world and taught biblical principles of intercession back in the 1970s that transformed the minds of believers. The teaching helped establish a biblical foundation and framework for a lifestyle of extended worship, prayer, and fasting to soon be welcomed by a generation. It also paved the way for greater revelation to come forth in the future.

David Yonggi Cho of South Korea carried a dream and built a prayer mountain that proved to be a sanctuary where individuals could hide away in small cubicles for periods of intense prayer and fasting. This was initially built in 1973 and later renovated in 1982 to accommodate over 10,000 people. Today millions of people continue to visit this renowned location and engage in 24/7 worship and prayer nearly four decades after it began! Pastor Cho also proved how sustained prayer and worship can completely revolutionize society and culture, as seen with the modern rise and economic success of South Korea.

Lou Engle was a simple man in Southern California leading small, poorly attended prayer meetings while paying the bills by mowing lawns. God began to ignite a dream in his heart to hold massive solemn assemblies according to the pattern of Joel 2 that would shift culture and call a nation back to God. After an incredible journey following the wind of God, the initial "TheCall" gathering was launched in the year 2000 in Washington, DC. As mentioned earlier, more than 450,000 burning hearts from across many denominations, streams, movements, and churches gathered in the Mall to cry out for revival on behalf of America. At 16 years old, I was among the masses that day and was marked forever by that strategic event. A significant shift took place across America that I believe even turned the tide of the elections that took place that fall.

Pete Grieg from 24/7 prayer wrote a prayer titled "the vision" late one night on the wall of an underground prayer room in England. The words leaked out the next morning and ignited fresh faith, hope, and perseverance in the hearts of countless people with the same passion. The message spread like wildfire and virally infected thousands and millions! I do not know of a single person in the worship and prayer movement who has not been completely rearranged by these words! "The Vision" brought much needed language and articulation to a generation for what God was doing with this rumbling across the earth.[1] Pete continues to stir hearts today with the books he writes and the 24/7 prayer movement he leads with hundreds of prayer rooms across the world.

Mike Bickle has implemented and facilitated a world-renowned model of night-and-day prayer and worship in Kansas City, Missouri, at the International House of Prayer. Mike also carries an ability to train a generation to keep the sustained fire burning through growing in the knowledge of God. The Lord has used him to catalyze the movement and mandate of restoring David's tent to the forefront of the church agenda worldwide. He is literally witnessing the vision God gave him in the 1980s—that the face of the church would be transformed in just one generation—become reality.

Many more pioneers, leaders, prophets, and Davidic hearts dotting the globe have blazed this trail we are humbly following. It is an honor and privilege to be living in a generation with so many fathers and mothers who have courageously and fearlessly carried the torch onward!

Divine Acceleration

As a result of the blood, sweat, tears, and vision of these trail blazers and countless others throughout history, breakthrough is taking place. In accordance with the season of divine acceleration that is preparing the way for the return of Christ to the earth, this global movement of worship and prayer is stronger now than it has ever been in the history of humanity.

Today, there are thousands upon thousands of furnaces, houses of prayer, and worship gatherings in virtually every nation and region of the world. Millions are gathering every week around the globe to facilitate these furnaces and prayer rooms. Gone are the days of the empty, stale, and dilapidated worship and prayer gatherings as this new move is marked by a prophetic and spontaneous flow of worship, fiery prayers, intercession, radical fasting, and mass corporate agreement that moves Heaven and changes earth.

Whether it's on the 58th floor of a Manhattan skyscraper in New York City, a bamboo thatched roof hut in the jungles of Borneo, Indonesia, a basement in the desert of Northern Iraq, or a café located on the downtown strip of Perth, Australia, the Tabernacle of David is being rebuilt in our day. This fragrance of night-and-day worship is bringing forth divine transformation and salvation on the earth. What was prophesied and promised in Malachi 1:11 is coming to fulfillment in our day.

The Wildfire

What is coming next is only an increase and acceleration of what is already taking place. We are witnessing an amazing rate of growth that cannot be contained, categorized, or counted!

The Lord spoke to me about this very early on, in the first year the Burn movement began to really ignite all over America. Expansion was occurring at such a rapid pace that cities and nations all over the world began to start a "Burn furnace" without even being connected with our leaders. The fire was spreading, the word was getting out—and I was frustrated.

I had a growing concern about the consistency of the movement under such a sporadic and wild explosion of growth. This especially was true around the world as I did not have the relational connection or depth with many of the new leaders popping up all over the place. I began to share my frustration with the Lord and He exposed the control gripping my own heart and keeping me back from entering fully into the inferno He was lighting.

In our conversation, I plainly told the Lord: "It has gotten too big, too messy, and is too unorganized. We do not know our leaders as well as I really want to, and I'm worried that we are losing our consistency as more people groups, cities, and nations get involved." Then I drew it to a conclusion with this line: "It has become a wildfire that no one can contain!"

I instantly heard the audible voice of the Lord reply, "That is exactly the way I like it, Sean."

The time of Christ's coming is closer than it has ever been, and every nation, tribe, and tongue is strategically taking her place to beckon Him back! You and I are part of that army and joining in that song. This movement and holy synergy surrounding the rebuilding of David's tent is picking up steam like never before. The Kingdom of God is being established in our hearts and on the earth as He is being enthroned on the praises of His people as Psalm 22:3 promises. The coming of this Kingdom through perpetual, consistent, and fiery night-and-day worship and prayer is leading to the greatest harvest of souls the world has yet seen.

Endnote

1. See "The Words of the Vision," www.24-7prayer.ca/index.
php?itemid=24&catid=5. Accessed May 18, 2010.

6

A NEW SOUND FOR A NEW DAY

This overwhelming move of God's presence is carrying a fresh sound that is unlike anything history has ever heard before. The most significant revivals, renewals, awakenings, and moves of God throughout history have all been characterized by the sound that accompanied them. This sound captured the movement of God and sonically displayed what was taking place in that particular season. Today is a new season, and therefore it demands the release of a new sound.

The Sounds of History

A perfect example of the sound capturing what God was doing in the season can be seen by looking at the world-renowned Welsh

Revival. This revival, which exploded in 1904, lasted 18 months, and resulted in the salvation of over 300,000 souls, is still commonly referred to as the "singing revival" in Wales today. Last year, I visited Moriah Chapel where a handful of praying teenagers helped ignite this fire and got seriously messed up (in a good way of course). Toward the back of the small chapel room are stacks upon stacks of songbooks jam-packed with lyrics of spontaneous songs and hymns that once flooded the airwaves of the meetings. There was a sound associated with that explosive move of God and it is scribed in those books. Many of the meetings were actually guided by the spontaneous and prophetic songs that came forth, whether they were sounds of healing, restoration, repentance, intimacy, or joy.

Then there was the legendary Moravians in Herrnhut, Germany, who hosted a prayer meeting that lasted over 120 years. They were also famed for the sound of their mobile prayer and worship gatherings. They are another excellent example of a new sound that embodied the new move of God. Oftentimes their unprompted gatherings took place in the church, on the streets of the city, or even in the middle of the forest! They sang the hymns of the day so loudly many times during their dawn prayer meetings that it beckoned others to come and join in. It was like a morning wake-up call and alarm for the city! One could come to the conclusion that a new sound with both the Welsh and the Moravians brought in a new season of breakthrough, revival, and the power of God.

Yet again, the most significant event after the resurrection in the New Testament was also characterized by a sound. On obeying the last words of Jesus to "wait for the gift my Father promised," the hungry gathered in the upper room in Acts 2 worshiping, praying, and fasting for several weeks.

*Suddenly **a sound** like the blowing of a violent wind came from heaven and filled the whole house where they were sitting* (Acts 2:2 NIV).

I often imagine what the sound that came from that room was like. Worship, intercession, the blowing wind of Heaven, and the flames of fire were all mingled together in one explosive roar signaling the coming of the Holy Spirit to rest among men! Also, take note of what gathered the curious crowd to come and experience the "shock and awe" of this moment: *"When they heard **this sound**, a crowd came together in bewilderment…"* (Acts 2:6 NIV).

It was this sound that captivated a lost generation and called them into beholding this new frequency. As they came in deeper and gathered from all walks of life, they received salvation and followed Jesus.

Zeal Is Here

Just as the past moves of God's Spirit throughout history were recognized for their unique sound, a new and fresh sound is being released that is ushering in this new season on the earth. This emerging sound has less to do with a new style, genre, guitar reverb, or a musical fad and more accurately represents an awakening of hunger, passion, and desire from the depths of our hearts. *"Deep calls unto deep"* (see Ps. 42:7) as this outburst of authentic and radical zeal that has been dormant for too long is unleashed for the world to hear.

Do not mistake or confuse this sound with hype or manipulation. It is the undignified shout of praise rising from the depths of our beings to fully express and give glory, honor, and power where it is due! It is a prophetic sound of faith partnering with the heart of God that *"calls those things that do not exist as though they did"* (Rom. 4:17). It is a sound that is louder, stronger, and more powerful than the pessimistic and negative noise of the age. In its frequencies are faith, hope, love, and life made accessible to all who hear it. This sound has already begun taking over the airwaves and will continue getting louder and louder as the day of the coming of the Lord quickly approaches.

A Sound to the Barrenness

At the start of every New Year, our Burn 24-7 tribe leaders, musicians, and "burners" from more than 90 cities around the world join together in a corporate fast for at least a week. The purpose of this fast is to posture our global leaders in a place of consecration where we can seek God for direction, guidance, and vision for the coming season. It is always a powerful time for me personally as I am saturated in heavy revelation that sets my spirit on track for the coming year.

About halfway through the fast this past year, I became overwhelmed with the broken, disillusioned, and shattered state of my nation, the United States of America. This made such a deep impact on my spirit that a sense of hopelessness and unease filled my heart. In the midst of the great movement God has been releasing across the nation, all I could think of was the extreme barrenness over the land. I was reminded of the sobering statistics and staggering trends that reveal the depth of the moral depredation we are experiencing as millions from my generation are drowning in their own disillusionment and a cesspool of perversion.

This feeling rarely falls on me in this way. I really consider myself an optimist. I know that God never releases these sober revelations without having a solution already in place, but I did not behold any solutions in that moment. This slammed me as a pulsating, travailing, aching feeling that launched me into intense and immediate intercession. I actually thought I could feel a fraction of the pain in God's heart as He wept over the nation.

I began praying for the Burn furnaces we have tirelessly planted across America in the past three years. I saw the pictures of the directors in each city courageously and relentlessly gathering their tribes together to release incense that would flood the streets, homes, churches, schools, businesses, and bars. I saw the young and old joined together on their faces at midnight on Friday night in makeshift prayer rooms using churches, storefronts, and even pubs. I heard their songs and prayers exalting and enthroning God while asking for a move of love to bring unity, peace, and passion to their cities. They were asking for a move that confronts apathetic and complacent religion and beckons for the sons and daughters of God to be revealed according to Romans 8:19.

As I prayed, I saw a crazy, young, longhaired hippie band strumming three chords while they took their place as the watchmen on the wall at 2:30 A.M. No one was even in the room and even the soundman had gone to sleep, but an audience of One who never sleeps was watching. While everyone else in the city slept and slumbered, they contended, burned, and enjoyed God's presence.

Then the Lord spoke to me in an ever-so-powerful, majestic, soft, authoritative, yet kind voice:

> *"This is your season to sing over the barrenness of the land…and watch it come to life."*

I came undone and began to weep at hearing these words. Isaiah

54:1 was immediately brought to my attention as prophecy for this season in my nation.

> *"Sing, O barren woman, you who never bore a child; burst into song, shout for joy, you who were never in labor; because more are the children of the desolate woman than of her who has a husband," says the Lord* (Isaiah 54:1 NIV).

Coming Alive

In the weeks that followed, God began to open my eyes during times of worship and I saw things that I have never seen before. As we began to worship during burn sets, conferences, and church services, I could see heaviness, oppression, and barrenness over hearts and lives as they first entered the room and readied themselves for a dutiful "religious exercise." Though it was a bit intense to have eyes now to see this taking place in the spirit, a beautiful transformation was about to take place! It is interesting to me that when we are living in times of struggle, lack, and disappointment, the Bible only points to one acceptable and appropriate response: SING!

As we entered into His Presence, I strongly encouraged those in the corporate body who felt this heaviness on them to sing and flood the atmosphere with their sounds of worship, praise, and prophetic proclamation. I could see the frequencies and melodies of Heaven surge through bodies as they joined in the song of the angels, elders, and all of creation. The breath of God was releasing life back into these broken people and they were literally "coming alive" as we got deeper and deeper into realms of His glory together. Hope, dreams, life, faith, and fresh energy were restored as this sound went forth! The Book of James teaches us that life and death are in the power of the tongue (see James 3:2-12). When we release this sound of life, faith, and hope from our mouths, we can actually prophesy ourselves, our families, cities, and nations into a new season of fullness and restoration! Is that not incredible to comprehend? What a beautiful truth of this new prophetic sound God is restoring on our lips!

Fresh Faith for a New Day

These experiences have restored hope, vision, and fire into my bones to release new songs in this hour that call the dead things to come back to life. God released a mandate on us during that annual global fast to release and spread this sound of awakening all across the nations of the earth. This actually spawned the biggest, most expansive recording project of my entire life entitled "Rebirth and Reclamation." The project was an experiment, and unlike any of the previous nine albums I had produced and recorded. We used several unconventional and fresh methods, with the goal of crafting a sound that would carry fresh faith for a new day. The producers, musicians, and engineers all agreed they had to meticulously ensure that every tone, inflection, melody, rhythm, and frequency truly carried a sound and spirit of resurrection life.

Many of us have allowed the voice of the liberal media and secular society to infiltrate our minds, homes, families, and churches for too long. These worldly voices have been used to prophesy discouragement, strife, recession, fear, and panic while the Church was meant to set the tone with a clarion sound of life! This new sound of faith already being released carries confidence and courage and is inviting music to the ears of the world. In order to gain the renewed perspective from where this sound is birthed, we must *"come up here"* as the Spirit summoned John in Revelation 4. We can no longer sing, worship, pray, or prophecy from our current fleshly perspective of fear, but it must come from a higher place. The song will rise according to our measure of faith as mentioned in Romans 12:6. This method, mind-set, and renewed perspective is already beginning to spur on great testimonies of breakthrough across the world.

Transformation in the Red Light District

A few years ago, God began to burden our hearts for the red light districts of the nations. It was a theme that kept coming up during the late night worship sets in many of our furnaces around the world. Asking God for the ability to feel and know the feelings of His heart is actually a very dangerous prayer! What happens when He really begins to answer it?

I distinctly remember the night my wife received a massive impartation from God on behalf of the child prostitution and sex trade. This all happened in the middle of the night during a burn session in east Texas. The burden and heart of God fell on her like a bomb during worship and she was catapulted into almost instantaneous intercession, weeping, and heavy travail. This would be one of the most significant encounters of her life that would mark her for eternity.

Even as the current generation is more captivated and moved on behalf of social justice than many previous generations, many times the feeling comes from pity and not true unction and deposit from the heart of God. This produces actions and responses that lack sustaining and powerful answers or solutions. Only from the place of intimacy and pressing into the heart of God can we acquire His feelings and discover the divine strategy to release true justice on the earth. Authentic intimacy propels us forward into true advocacy that carries far more weight and authority than mere pity. As I, my wife, and several other leaders from Burn 24-7 have experienced similar encounters where we left undone, we have been moved from the place of His Presence to administrate and release justice to the oppressed, healing to the sick, and salvation to the lost.

It's the Sound of Justice

Not long after this encounter, we commissioned a team of burning hearts to respond to the crisis and devastation within the nation of Uganda in east Africa. The cries from those bound in poverty and disease and the thousands of children being raised up to be killers and soldiers in the rebel army reached the ears of the Lord. He shared His heart of compassion with us. We responded. The team descended on the nation with swift justice through cultivating night-and-day worship for three days nonstop. We also brought food, clothes, and blankets to the widows and orphans, administered medicine, and prayed over the sick and diseased. It was a phenomenal trip that opened our eyes to how God could use the blend of worship, prayer, and outreach to change cities and nations! The testimonies of salvations, healings, deliverances, and city transformation are absolutely incredible and faith building.

As we were booking tickets for our Burn Uganda team, I felt led to purposefully plan a 14-hour layover in Amsterdam on their return trip home. The team was not too happy with me as it was November in Europe and they were dressed for 90-plus degree weather near the equator in Africa! Even though they didn't understand and thought it was another one of my crazy ideas, they pressed onward. After arriving very early into Amsterdam's Schipol Airport from an overnight flight from Kampala, Uganda, they caught the first train and headed downtown in their flip-flops and shorts while carrying all their instruments. They responded to a clear word God gave me to simply find the biggest brothel in the middle of the Red Light District, burn with their instruments, and release a prophetic sound of worship that would flood the streets.

The Key of David

The team soon found a great corner to set up on and let it fly! They worshiped, prophesied, and sang out the cry of Jesus: *"Your Kingdom Come, Your will be done on earth as it is in Heaven."* This new prophetic, creative, and unhindered sound was loosed as the frequencies of faith filled the heavy air of the Red Light District. A sound went forth from the barrenness of those streets and into the hearts of the people aimlessly searching for meaning, hope, and value in life. The team saw nothing miraculous or supernatural take place in that moment, although they could sense a shift in the spirit. A few kind bystanders on the street tossed some change into their guitar cases, and they used the money to catch a train back to the airport in order to make their flight back to the States.

A few weeks later, one of the leaders of the team called me in shock and amazement. He was watching a special on a news program covering a story of how the Dutch government randomly closed down one of the biggest brothels in the Red Light District of Amsterdam. It is very unlikely and uncommon for this to happen, as even the prostitutes are taxed and the nation relies heavily on this income to maintain its budget. The news report began to divulge details about how the government invaded the brothel as they were shutting it down. As they peered inside, they soon discovered some of the most unimaginable things that were taking place. Little boys and girls from the Middle East and Asia were found trapped in sex slavery with no way out. Hearing this unfold, we were going ballistic and praising God! He granted justice as the team was on the street weeks before asking for God's Kingdom to be established in the city through this new sound.

The program then flashed pictures on the screen of the exact brothel that was shut down—it was the very same building that they were camped in front of and prophesying to from that street corner a few weeks earlier! As the worship, prayers, and new sound was unleashed from that place, principalities were shaken, demonic doors were shut, and true transformation took place! The key of David spoken of in Isaiah 22:22 was released through the sound, *"What he opens no one can shut, and what he shuts no one can open."*

This fresh sound from Heaven is carrying new measures of authority to release faith, stir up zeal, and establish the Kingdom of Heaven on the earth! Our songs and prayers over these cities are now saturated in confidence and faith from the power of His Presence to proclaim: "As it is in Heaven, so shall it be in the red light districts of the world!"

The Sound Is Here

This new sound arising is already starting to call forth a new season on the earth. It's a sound of life, resurrection, rebirth, and reclamation and a season of breakthrough, fire, and salvation. There is a sound of renewed innocence and faith that God is longing to release through His Body in this hour over the barrenness of our churches, cities, regions, and nations. The sound is awakening prodigal sons and daughters to throw off their grave clothes and enter into the promises of God during this hour in history! The sound is also being sung to the barrenness of our own hearts, dreams, and lives and beckoning us to birth new life yet again. It is the sound coming forth as we gather in our cities and flood the air with perpetual and unending melodies and songs. It is a sound that is creative, intriguing, and inviting to every barren soul longing to be made fertile again.

7

THE POWER OF MY PRESENCE

L ast year, I was returning from a trip visiting one of our long-term Burn 24-7 mission teams located in the jungles of Borneo, Indonesia. They had been living there for six months contending for the soul of the largest Muslim nation in the world to turn to God. The ministry was incredibly full, nonstop, and taxing most days, but it is definitely the place where you want to be poured out like a drink offering. Indonesia is home to 23 unreached people groups representing millions upon millions who have still never heard the name of Jesus. I was looking forward to a quick stop in Sydney, Australia, on the way home for an extended weekend with hot showers, good friends, and a great time chasing after God together. After de-planing the overnight red-eye flight down to Australia, I ventured out into the beautiful city of Sydney to breathe in some fresh air before the meeting began that night. Little did I know that day God was going to bomb me with one of the most amazing encounters of my life.

I began to hike around the glorious trail from Bronte Bay to Bondi Beach and soak in the gorgeous scenery of the Sydney coast while adjusting to another time zone. The weather was breezy, cool, and dry as Australia was coming out of winter and welcoming the warmth of spring. It was an incredibly magnificent journey with winding trails and stunning views from the seaside cliffs.

As I continued walking, my fascination with the ocean grew incredibly strong. I was mesmerized and drawn into some sort of trance and became engrossed in the movement of the ocean taking place below. During this fixation, the Lord began to speak so clearly to me, "Look at the ocean." As I was peering out, I became overwhelmed with the raw powerful energy of the ocean as the waves pounded against the rock cliffs jutting out into the sea. The wind raging, the current swirling, and the waves mounting up created this psychotic pulsating rhythm of its own that was uncontrollable and untamable. It was an absolutely staggering moment of raw creation revealing its raw Creator.

I have never seen the ocean like it was that day! With all the swirling whitewash, it was even hard to see the actual turquoise-blue color hiding underneath. Even at Australia's premier surfing hot spots along the coast, no one dared to get out in the swell this day. This surge began to even gain the attention of nearby tourists, as they could not help but gawk with amazed looks at the phenomena unfolding before their eyes.

His Response

The Lord began to speak to me again: "This is a picture of what the great end-time move of My presence will look like." I was baffled as I realized this was the answer to the question I had asked the Lord the day before. I was on a layover in Malaysia and decided to venture to the top of the downtown Menara Tower overlooking the vast Asian metropolis of Kuala Lumpur. While viewing the mosques littering the city as far as the eye could see, I was overcome with a longing more than ever to see the King return in all of His majesty to the billions of souls in the surrounding nations who had never heard the truth and were enshrouded in lies and deception.

In that moment my soul was filled with a passion I did not even know existed, and I shouted out, "When is this promised move of Your Spirit going to crash on these nations, and what will it look like?" I heard no response except a few strange looks from nearby locals gawking at this crazy white man. Not surprisingly, the lack of response did not disturb me, as it was a question one does not expect a response to. My limited understanding told me it was just another thing I would "figure out" or it would unfold before me as I kept pressing on. All this changed that day and in that moment.

The Overwhelming Move

As I continued to take in the panoramic of the raging ocean, the Spirit began to download on me the revelation of what was being spoken. I began to draw a parallel between the scene of this ocean and the coming move of God on the earth. I quickly understood this would be a fierce, violent, and offensive move unlike what I had ever experienced or expected. He spoke once again, "It's a move of the overwhelming **power** of My presence." I began to sense the raw surging power of the ocean grip my heart and felt the glory of God come all over me. I started to weep right there on the cliffs while watching this all unfold. He continued to speak: "It's a move that will stun and shock humanity as I pour out My Spirit on all flesh. Nothing will stop the deep waters of My presence as they wash over the nations."

I then began to physically shake uncontrollably as the images from the last week flooded my mind. The faces, smiles, and gestures of the villagers living in the deep jungles of Borneo began to flash through my memory. I knew that this next wave is something beyond what we have ever experienced in history. Above styles, fads, hype, giftings, or even anointings, the raw surging presence of God will take center stage. He is commanding complete control as we give Him room through surrendered hearts. This is an invitation to go deeper into the places we have never visited before. They are not ankle-deep wading waters of convenient Christianity, but as Ezekiel 47:5 articulates, they are ferocious waters to swim in that *"could not be crossed."*

The Sound of Rushing Waters

Then came the sound. The ear-splitting and roaring sound of the waters began to move me and surge through my soul. The ocean was raging and rumbling so loud that it made it hard to think at times. I began to reflect on a recent study of sound waves I had completed. The ocean noise and waterfalls are some of the only "sounds" on the earth literally fulfilling the entire sound spectrum. The sound frequencies audible to the human ear are between 20 and 20,000 hertz. Those frequencies below 20 hertz are actually felt more by the human body than they are heard. The frequencies above 20,000 could cause major hearing damage with prolonged exposure. The noise of this fierce riptide was accurately covering the entire grid of earthly sound frequency. This is similar to the sound coming from Heaven mentioned in Revelation 14:2: *"And I heard a sound from heaven like the roar of rushing waters and like a loud peal of thunder…"* (NIV).

The Spirit began speaking again by saying, "The nations will know My presence is coming as the sound comes forth from the waters." I was standing in shock as the thunderous ocean noise grew louder and louder to my ears. Revelation dawned that the endless hours of passionate and fiery worship and prayer that have been released in our cities around the world are beginning to usher in this move! It is that unified sound from the Bride mentioned at the end of the Book of Revelation that is signaling to the nations to get ready as, *"The Spirit and the Bride say, 'Come!'"* (Rev. 22:17 NIV).

With all this madness happening around me and the deep emotion being released from the inner core of my being, I frantically opened up my Bible to see if I could possibly find anything to bring confirmation or validation to all this. As I thumbed open the page, this was the very first line I read in that moment: *"You have overwhelmed me with all your waves"* (Ps. 88:7 NIV).

The Burn Wagon

Every summer, we send out young teams of fiery teenage worshipers, musicians, prophets, and intercessors across America for the most thrilling month-long road trip of their lives! About 20 to 30 young musicians, artists, intercessors, prophets, and revivalists pack into an old Greyhound-style bus emblazoned with freshly painted red flames on the side. Every day along their journey, they stop in a different city leading and facilitating explosive worship, prayer, and impartation gatherings. Many times they will lead all-night burn sessions of worship and prayer that last until the following morning.

They converge on a variety of different venues including churches, nightclubs, outdoor parks, and even street corners. No city is safe from the sound of passion welling up inside these young fiery "musicianaries"! Appropriately named the "Burn Wagon," they have quickly become known across America for their Holy Ghost antics and helping facilitate atmospheres of supernatural breakthrough.

Our initial experiment with this idea several years ago saw the Burn Wagon team conclude their journey on the streets of Times Square in downtown New York City. They made it a mission to find the busiest street corner possible where they busted out their guitars and hand drums to create a "resting place" and habitation for God in the middle of the chaos and confusion of Manhattan. Heaven began to kiss earth in the most unlikely of all places! As they continued releasing the sound and fragrance of worship, these fiery teens unleashed prayer and impartation on every passing bystander! A line was formed on each end of the sidewalk as random people began to pass through this "fire tunnel." Many were blasted and bombarded with the thick presence and glory of God! The hungry hearts received prayer and the hurting received healing as the revelation of God's nearness fell on the streets of New York City. This first experiment launching "Burn Wagon" proved successful and compelled us to send four more wagons the following year.

Sobered With Our Lack

Upon the teams' return home from their journeys, we love to hear, celebrate, and publish the most radical testimonies, stories, and memories from each trip. Signs and wonders, creative miracles, deliverances, and salvations have been commonplace among each of our Burn Wagon and global missions teams. It continually amazes me how these young revivalists are moving in such an incredible realm of power and authority at such young ages. I believe this all stems from a lifestyle saturated in endless hours of worship and prayer in His Presence.

There seems to be one common remark on the evaluations compiled upon return of these Burn Wagon teams. This consistent observation by these young "burners" is the sober realization of how barren and devoid much of America's churches are from the glory of His Presence resting in their midst. It is shocking for these young firebrands to comprehend being plugged into a community that does not foster "a resting place" as a core value and priority. After these gatherings, which consist of four simple chords on the guitar, a cry of desperation for God's face, and raspy, gut-wrenching prayers, these teenagers always provide the most interesting feedback.

Phone calls, emails, and letters pour into our headquarters office describing how people have never witnessed the same feeling of nearness as they did during the night our team visited. Many of these responses continue to ask the question, "Was that the presence of God I felt that night?" and, "Is that what He feels like?" We are so excited and thrilled that an encounter of this magnitude was experienced but are saddened that these occurrences are not yet commonplace in the responders' cities, communities, and homes. In the midst of so many programs, churches, strategies, and services, could we be missing out on the greatest treasure of all? How can a person attend church for so long and be in meetings for hours upon hours of their life and not experience the true presence of God in our day? We must do whatever it takes to welcome the power of His Presence back to our nations, cities, communities, and homes! It is our portion, inheritance, and reward.

Resting Place

This movement of the power of His Presence arising across the nations of the earth is far more than just a cool new religious or flashy form of godliness lacking true power. But we are literally coming together as the *"living stones"* referred to in First Peter 2:5 to build a dwelling for the presence of God. It is not a new ritual, fad, or some slick structure. Our lovesick worship and pursuit is creating a hotbed for the raw presence of God as He is *"enthroned in the praises"* of His people according to Psalm 22:3. From the establishment of His throne in our midst, genuine transformational power is made available to a broken humanity.

Ever since the fall of Adam and Eve in the Garden, God has been longing to restore that place of true communion and unity with Him. This is a common thread that weaves throughout every book, story, and principle in the Bible.

In Isaiah 66:1, God makes note of this with a question:

> *Heaven is My throne, and the earth is My footstool.*
> *Where is the house you will build for Me? Where will*
> *My resting place be?* (Isaiah 66:1 NIV)

Jesus also reiterates this theme in Matthew 8:20 when He bares His heart to the crowd following Him:

> *Foxes have holes and birds of the air have nests, but the Son of Man has no place to lay His head* (Matthew 8:20 NIV).

The longing of God's heart is to find people willing to position themselves in a posture to receive Him in all His glory. Most of the time, this requires a certain amount of inconvenience on our part, as He rarely fits into our schedules, paradigms, and preconceived ideas. Oh, but the reward is not even worth comparing to the sacrifice! When we invite the move of God in our lives, homes, and churches, we must understand that He comes to not "fit in" but to completely take over. The Book of Isaiah describes Him as the "All-Consuming Fire" and He comes to consume everything (see Isa. 10:17; 30:27; 33:14). He demands our full attention, full affection, and our entire lives. When we invite Him to come and rest in our midst, we are relinquishing our "control-freak" mentality and giving Him an "all-access" pass to completely rearrange our services, lives, and hearts.

Many churches, fellowships, and ministries across the Western world are barren and devoid of the true presence and power of God because they are simply not willing to make room to receive Him. Even though our churches may have large congregations, amazing programs, great sounding bands, stunning buildings, big budgets, and decent coffee, if we lack the raw power and glory of God resting in our midst, then it is all for naught. Just as Mary's womb made room to receive the gift of God's son, Jesus, our hearts must also make room. We are not smart, wise, rich, or crafty enough on our own to release true transformation, but we are totally dependent on His Presence. A dying world does not need our fancy buildings and programs. It needs to experience a life-altering encounter where people are marked by the glory of His Presence resting among them! As the world's citizens continue their quest to fill the ache in their hearts, we have the incredible privilege to host Him—the One who heals the heartaches—in our midst.

The Gift of Hospitality

The greatest opportunity is before the Church as we continue to gather and stoke the fire corporately around the world. We have a divine invitation to Host the very person of God every single time we gather together to worship. Can you believe that? The gift of hospitality is being stirred up in our hearts, homes, and cities as revelation dawns that we are hosting the King of Glory in our midst! The mentality is now being broken that we simply meet to fulfill a religious obligation and make ourselves feel better. We do not have time cards and God is not going to check how many punches are in our Sunday morning ticket at the pearly gates into Heaven. We are very familiar with the statement of Jesus in Matthew 18:20, *"Where two or three are gathered...I am in there in the midst of them."* We have quoted it, sung it, and memorized it. But do we really believe it? Has it, like many other powerful truths, been reduced down from authentic reality to Christian rhetoric?

Imagine that a distinguished guest of high stature was coming to stay for a night in your home. It could be a president, king, or high dignitary from a faraway land. You would begin preparing well in advance and make sure you have everything ready for his (or her) coming. The moment he arrives into your home, you would forsake everything else going on in your life in order to fully pay attention to him and fulfill every one of his desires. You would make it your top priority to make him feel comfortable, received, and at home during his stay with you.

It is no different than when we come together and invite the Person of God to rest in our midst. He is the guest of honor and the only One whose needs we are attending to. We must forsake everything else to simply pay attention to Him and serve the needs of His heart. I believe this is the shift that is taking place and beginning to mark our meetings with a stronger and weightier presence than we have ever known before.

Having traveled extensively around the world in many different nations, cities, and people groups, I have spent the night in homes, shacks, tents, hotels, and places that people would not believe. I have found out that you can learn so much about a culture by staying in a local person's home for a night. For this reason, I typically reject the option on many trips to default to a nice, Western, stale hotel in exchange for the uniqueness and warmth of a home. Jesus also instructed His disciples to travel from house to house as well, looking for the "man of peace."

On this journey of staying in homes across the world, it has been revealed how pathetically low I have valued hospitality, as shown by the time and energy I have invested, and how highly this principle is valued in many poorer nations of the world. I have been completely humbled in ways I cannot even express as my hosts in other nations have sacrificed literally everything for the sake of my comfort. It has moved me to do anything and everything in my power to return back time and time again to those nations, cities, and communities where I am truly welcomed.

I remember one example of this radical hospitality that took place on a trip a few years ago. I was staying in a quaint Himalayan village in the high peaks of Nepal. My hosts were former Tibetan Buddhist monks who carried a powerful testimony of how Jesus appeared to them one afternoon during their duties in the temple. This encounter compelled them to spread the truth of Jesus—and entire villages were getting saved! One thing these people know about Americans is that we love Coca-Cola. Upon my arrival at their humble village home with a thatched roof, they immediately sent someone on a strenuous four-hour roundtrip hike to buy a drink in the next village! When I discovered the extent of their sacrifice and willingness to serve at such an inconvenient level, the warm soda was a sign of honor that humbled me to no end.

Becoming a Bethany

I believe this is the very characteristic that marked the city of Bethany in the Bible. Jesus had a fixation with this tiny town outside of Jerusalem. There was something magnetic about this "off the beaten path" place that attracted the attention of Jesus. He was known for stopping through many times, performing stunning miracles (and possibly His most dynamic miracle of raising Lazarus from the dead), and even spending the night here throughout His earthly ministry. This is also the location where the notorious anointing of Jesus' feet with the costly perfume by Mary of Bethany took place. This humble town put into practice the gift of hospitality to where even the Son of God was moved and could not stay away! Just imagine how learning this key principle could beckon in the greatest sustaining move of God's presence we have ever witnessed in our communities, cities, and nations!

During one of our large Burn 24-7 worship events last year, the Lord spoke the exact same words and released the same vision on the same night to many of our leaders. It was one of those crazy, wild, freakish experiences you could not even make up if you wanted to!

During the vision, the Lord spoke these simple yet profound words: "I am looking for a people that will simply pay attention to me." These words catapulted us on a deeper journey to do just that. Instead of just organizing, mobilizing, and expending ourselves to lead a movement of worship, prayer, and missions while getting caught in the "busyness" of ministry, we had to make radical lifestyle changes and reprioritize our own lives. Many of us even transformed entire rooms in our homes into sacred spaces where we can do nothing but "waste" time paying attention to Him. It brought an entire shift to the Burn 24-7 movement to truly practice and implement what we preach and believe.

The Dream

What if we placed the priority of Him actually "resting" in our midst higher than anything else? What could happen if we reshaped our meetings to accommodate and welcome Him rather than catering to everyone else in attendance? Couldn't He then come and meet the needs of every person in the room? If God is truly looking for a place to dwell and desiring to find a people to rest among, then what could happen if we literally took Him at His word and made room? This paradigm shift is needed now more than ever, and will bring the needed shift to our churches, services, homes, families, and lives. It is not a new strategy by any means, but simply a returning to the "ancient paths," as described in Jeremiah 6:16.

The power of His Presence is defining this overwhelming move already crashing on the shores of the nations! The world is recognizing the move of the Gospel once again not just for its buildings, television programs, language, and rhetoric, but for its undeniable power. The Church is transitioning into her finest hour and truly embodying First

Corinthians 4:20, which states, *"The Kingdom of God is not a matter of talk, but of power"* (NIV). Are not our lives, cities, nations, and everything else transformed as He dwells and stays with us? Is not one moment in His Presence much better than hours upon hours of boring and monotonous religious exercise? What are we waiting for, then? We have been dreaming of a day that is already upon us! This is a day where we no longer rely on the entanglements, forms, and crafty strategies. It is a day where we forsake everything else for the pursuit of His overwhelming presence. He alone is the strategy! He alone is our source!

8

RELEASING THE FRAGRANCE

D ay-and-night worship and prayer is filling the heavens like never before in history. Never has there been such a widespread momentum on the global Church prioritizing the presence of God in worship, intercession, and encounter! It can easily be stated that more people are postured in the place of intercession than at any other time. All you have to do is type *house of prayer* into an Internet search engine to realize that God is doing this all over the world and at a rate that we cannot even keep up with.

At the same time, more and more people are feeling called to leave their "homes" and journey to a distant land to take the Gospel to some of the hardest and darkest places on the planet. The current missions thrust will easily go down as the largest in history. The uniqueness of this thrust is that the Western church no longer fuels it, as it had for the last 1,000 years. The largest number of Christians in any one country is now in China, with well over 120 million believers. The single largest church in the world is found in Korea. Although nobody seems to completely agree on which nation has the fastest-growing population of Christianity, all the top competitors reside in Asia. Such nations as China, India, and Nepal top this list! The Gospel is moving forward like never before in history. With renewed enthusiasm, the church is looking at where we are not, rather than staying focused on where we are. As technologies like the 4K map and unity movements like the Call2All network continue to move forward, so does the recognition of where the greatest needs are. With this is coming a renewed passion to strategically release resources into these regions to see the completion of the Gospel being shared in every tribe, tongue, and nation.

A Year of Jubilee

As I write this, I am sitting in a hotel room in a small, relatively unknown nation that will have to remain anonymous for security reasons. I first came to this country four years ago and did not meet a single believer. As I walked the land and prayed, I immediately felt the Lord shackling my heart to the future of this nation and I gladly submitted. Each year, I have made a trip back to this nation and each year the doors have opened wider to pour into the underground church and encourage the move of God here. In 2007, as I realized this nation was coming up on 50 years of Christian history within its borders, the Lord began to impress on my heart that the nation was soon going to be experiencing its Jubilee year. In addition, He began to show me that in biblical history, God would supply three times the harvest in the year leading up to the Jubilee (see Lev. 25:21). This was in order to provide the necessary food to last through the jubilee while the land rested from planting.

I began to share with local leaders at that time that I felt the Lord was going to be releasing unprecedented harvest. I shared with them that I felt that before long, they would be experiencing the liberty and rightful release of inheritance that the Jubilee represented in Israel's history. Over the last three years, I have watched as the numbers of Christians has more than doubled in the nation! And for the first time in 100 years of nationhood, the prime minster has declared that it is legal to be Christian! I believe the full release of the Jubilee is still coming and that this nation is just at the beginning of a huge harvest of souls that will number in the tens of thousands. Clearly God is on the move! The believers still face many different forms of persecution, especially in the villages. I believe the Jubilee will be fully expressed when public worship takes place on the streets as the Christians are freed to celebrate their love for Jesus without any restrictions.

This is only one example of a host of testimonies from what God is doing all over the world. Truly we live in unprecedented days!

Revival Is in the Air

No longer do we need to say that we are crying out for a revival that we are not yet seeing. It is already upon us!

This last year, my friend Taylor and I took a 12-hour train ride from western Germany down to southern Germany for a two-hour-long meeting with a hero of the faith in Germany. This man has spent the last 40-plus years of his life contending for revival in Germany and abroad. For the last 30 years, he has committed himself to pray for God to raise up 100 revivalists and 100 reformers that would change the world. John Wesley is said to have proclaimed that a hundred men who fear nothing but God and hate nothing but sin could set the world on fire. We received an invitation to make a quick trip to have this man share his heart and pray for us. We jumped at the opportunity to have a man of this caliber lay hands and impart his heart for revival to us. I am unapologetically after authentic revival and feel no pride in saying that I long to be a vessel unto that purpose! Just 24 hours on a train is a small price to pay to glean a few pearls from a man who has invested so much in the Kingdom.

One of my questions to him was, "What must we do to see revival?" His reply was exactly what I was hoping to hear. He looked at us with tremendous assurance and through a translator declared, "Revival is already in the air." I could feel the electricity on this statement! It struck my spirit like a bolt of lightning, igniting a further baptism of confidence that the tide of revival is already surging ahead!

But still the question remains valid. What must we do to see the further release of this revival all over the world? A great revivalist of the nineteenth century, Charles Finney, believed that revival was not just a sovereign act of God alone with no interplay of man. Rather, Finney confronted the apathy of his day by declaring that one must pray down revival. Many wanted to sit back and blame the lack of spiritual momentum on a lack of God desiring to pour it out. Finney records in his memoirs the type of spiritual violence he believed released revival:

> I found myself so much exercised, and so borne down with
> the weight of immortal souls that I was constrained to pray
> without ceasing. Some of my experiences, indeed, alarmed

me. A spirit of importunity sometimes came upon me so that I would say to God that He had made a promise to answer prayer, and I could not, and would not, be denied. I felt so certain that He would hear me, and that faithfulness to His promises, and to Himself, rendered it impossible that He should not hear and answer, that frequently I found myself saying to Him, "I hope thou dost not think that I can be denied, I come with thy faithful promises in my hand, and I cannot be denied." I cannot tell how absurd unbelief looked to me, and how certain it was in my mind, that God would answer prayer—those prayers that, from day to day, and from hour to hour, I found myself offering in such agony and faith. I had no idea of the shape the answer would take, the locality in which the prayers would be answered, or the exact time of the answer. My impression was that the answer was near, even at the door; and I felt myself strengthened in the divine life, put on the harness for a mighty conflict with the powers of darkness, and expected soon to see a far more powerful outpouring of the Spirit of God, that new country where I had been laboring.[1]

Oh that we would be filled with such surety and confidence! God truly wants to baptize His insecure Bride in a deluge of confidence, hope, and faith that His glory is prevailing over every bit of darkness. Once again, we can see that this missions explosion we are now experiencing, and will experience in even greater ways, is completely connected to laboring in intimacy-based prayer and contending for the purposes of God to be poured out. From this place comes the confidence to walk among the poor, broken, rich, apathetic, deceived, and with fiery love filling our hearts, see light break in again and again!

This is where a missions explosion in every sphere of life becomes a nonnegotiable reality through the global Church. Missions becomes what we do at our workplace, what we do in our neighborhoods, and what we do as we obey the call of God on our lives. This call may lead us to the slums of Calcutta, the high Himalayas of Nepal, the Red Light District of Amsterdam, the remote villages of the Amazon, the bustling cities of China, the studios of Hollywood, or any other unreached tribe, tongue, nation, sphere, or area of injustice! As we look at the early signs of revival in our times, we should be more inspired than ever to see this move of God go to the deepest echelons of every society and furthest corners of the earth. Through this baptism of confidence wrought in the place of prayer and intimacy, we will awaken to the reality that we are the fulfillment of the glory of the Lord being poured out all over the earth. *"For it is the God who commanded light to shine out of darkness, who has shone in our hearts to give the light of the knowledge of the glory of God in the face of Jesus Christ"* (2 Cor. 4:6). As He shines on our hearts, we shine on the world, and the Kingdom that is "in us" is released everywhere we go. We are waking up to the reality that whenever we step out our front door, glory has arrived on the streets. Whenever we step off a plane, glory has arrived in the region. No matter how dark or hard it may be, this confident Bride filled with the power and glory of God will prevail.

Serving With Love

The two absolute nonnegotiable aspects of this next missions movement are love and power. First and foremost, this move of God will be completely rooted in a Mary-type devotion that we see displayed in Luke 10:38-42. This story is all too familiar to us. Still in many ways, it can be easily misinterpreted. Many times we have heard the Mary and Martha comparison being between one who sits at the feet of Jesus in prayer and worship and one who is "overly busy" in serving Jesus. Time and time again, we have been exhorted to just sit at His feet and stop being so busy. We do need to hear this from time to time. Yet, I don't believe this to be the primary message of the story. The key to understanding Martha's error is the phrase at the beginning of verse 40, which says, "*Martha was **distracted** with much serving*" (emphasis mine). It was not the fact that she was serving that was wrong, but rather, that she was distracted with her serving. This word *distracted* could literally be translated as being "driven out mentally" or "too busy." Jesus goes on to say that she is "*worried and troubled about many things.*" When looking into the Greek, this could read that Martha was "seeking her own agenda." Jesus' gentle rebuke had nothing to do with serving or not serving, but everything to do with the priority in her heart and mind. Martha had allowed herself to be driven out from His Presence mentally though still in the room physically. She had given herself to being overly busy, and she was literally after her own agenda.

Unfortunately this can be a major cause of burnout in missions and serving God in general. An absolute essential to a life of radical service, stirring revival, and lasting for the long haul will be the exact opposite of Martha's mistake: minds, hearts, and eyes fixed on Jesus even in the midst of serving—the priority of literal and spiritual rest; the laying aside of our agendas for the cause of the Kingdom. Lovers always make the best workers! Lovers will go to great lengths to serve the one they love the most. There are no time cards for lovers, no office hours, no retirement, but rather a sheer determination, in intimacy, to express love back to the One who loved us first.

Love-Filled Power

The second nonnegotiable in this current move of God is that we must be a people who unapologetically hunger for the power of God! Anything less is a partial Gospel and misrepresentation of the very core of God's nature and character. He is completely, utterly, and infinitely supernatural. He does not know how to be anything but supernatural. It is His supernatural power that created everything that exists, holds all things together, and sustains life on the earth. It has conquered sin and death; saved our souls, spirits, and bodies; and given us the power to overcome and the power to live by the same Spirit that did all these things. It is time to stop apologizing for our need for power in the Christian life and resolve to live as Paul admonishes us in First Corinthians 14:1. Paul says to *"eagerly desire the spiritual gifts"* (NIV). It is time to give up powerless Christianity and step into the promise of Jesus that we would walk in *"greater works than these"* (see John 14:12). It is time to perform the works of God, in the ways of God, full of the Heart of God!

Just last week, one of our outreach teams targeted one of the largest gatherings of satan worshipers and occult members in Salem, Massachusetts, on Halloween night. This team spent hours in worship and intercession, getting totally saturated in the presence of God before hitting the streets. The results speak for themselves. Over 40 people were healed on the spot. Moreover, 12 people who came with allegiance to darkness left paying homage to the one true King! Glory stepped out on the streets! The stories could go on and on and are becoming more and more frequent all the time. These stories are not limited to one region of the world but are happening all over the earth. God is pouring out His Spirit. Part of successful missions in the future will be walking in the supernatural as if it were totally natural. Because it is!

Of course we can never seek God's power more than God Himself. We are about Jesus and Jesus is about His power being released. The Church must begin to realize that when we seek God, He comes with His power! Signs will begin to follow us like never before as we begin to expect them and take the risks necessary to see signs released. We need to learn to cultivate an expectancy for the supernatural, not just for cool testimonies, but because God receives great glory through His power-filled Bride!

Witnesses

I want to close this chapter by issuing a strong call to GO! Pray and go! Go and pray! Walk in love-filled power and power-filled love. Nations, tribes, tongues, and our neighbors cry out all over the earth for a witness to come who knows the One true God. In Acts 1:8 Jesus says:

> *But you shall receive power when the Holy Spirit has come upon you; and you shall be witnesses to Me in Jerusalem, and in all Judea and Samaria, and to the end of the earth* (Acts 1:8).

This word *witnesses* in the Greek is *martus*. This is the root word that we have used for the English word *martyr*. Jesus makes this statement on the heels of the disciples' question about restoring a literal kingdom in Israel. His response is to bring them back to their primary job description: "Be witnesses of what you have seen in Me, what you have experienced in walking with Me. And by the way, be willing to die for this message!" Sometimes we can get so caught up on our predictions of His return that we forget to actually be the witnesses He has called us to be!

Later on in Acts 22:15, as Paul shares his testimony, he states that he had been called to be a witness of the things he had seen and heard. I tell you, God is raising up witnesses all across the earth who will stand with fire in their bones, unable and unwilling to keep in the witness of the One they are seeing and hearing. Our personal intimacy spills out to become His global glory!

Endnote

1. Charles Finney, *Memoirs* (Grand Rapids, MI: Zondervan, 1989), 142-143.

9

AUTHENTIC COMMUNITY

The sound of damp wood crackling in the warm woodstove and the coolness of the outside air pressing in on the frosted windows produced an ambiance of comfort and rest. Our small team, much more like a family, consisted of five adults, two small children, and two overstuffed, weary cars filled with the majority of all that we owned. We were on the road trip of a lifetime about to enter into yet another life-shaping conversation! However, before we jump into the conversation, this road trip has a bit of history.

Six months previous to this, each of us had gone through a process of handing over the responsibilities that we had been carrying with a clear sense from the Lord that there was something new coming. We had felt the Lord say that if we would give Him 30 days of nothing more than seeking His face, it could determine the next 30 years. This was not the kind of word that we wanted to risk missing.

Perspective

We had established deep relationship over the last number of years and had even come to the place where, although we did not know what was next, we were determined to do it together. For 30 days we gathered in great anticipation of hearing the Lord release the most earth-shaking vision the world had ever seen. However, each day we met, prayed, worshiped, soaked, and studied, just to go home at the end of the day feeling a little bit more lost as to what God was trying to say. All we kept hearing was this word: *perspective.* But what did that have to do with vision? I want to change the world! However, this word would take us on a four-month life-changing adventure that has easily set us on a course for at least the next 30 years, if not more like 50 or 70. On that journey we would learn much more about each other than even how to change the world, and in that, maybe one of the greatest keys to true and lasting transformation. Authentic community.

On that chilly, fall day we found ourselves surrounded by the beauty of rural Washington state. We were being hosted by a small community whose inception had been around a vision to create a community where God's presence would be free to rest. They had formed around an adherence to the Constitution of God's written Word, a longing to see the Kingdom exemplified in an entire community, and a desire to inspire the nation back to its roots and into even greater future glory. We were going home to home, meeting with everyone we could to try and extract the truths they had been living for many years. Our little brains were being radically impacted by a lifestyle few of us had ever seen before. We walked by one man's home as he pointed out that all the concrete, rebar, and framing had been built so that this home would easily still be standing in 300 years. This building reflected a nonnegotiable principle in the community to make every decision, whether in the business, church, civil, or family sphere, in light of the next three generations. We heard many stories of the community coming together to rebuild burnt-down homes, reach out to each other's children, and fight for the destinies on the lives of those around them.

Plus Factor

As lunch wrapped up, the family hosting us began to pray and prophesy over us as they sought the Lord for the pearls of wisdom He would have them impart to us. I will never forget the simple but powerful word they gave us. It was the image of a crew of rowers in a boat race. As the boat smoothly glided through the water it began to pick up speed. The rowers started to all pull with the same strength, timing, and efficiency. The boat actually began to lift out of the water to a place where just the bottom keel remained in the water. The term for this is called the *plus factor* and it only happens as the rowers enter into true unity. The word for us was that God wanted to teach us about true community, which literally means "communing in unity." What emerged in each of our hearts as we contemplated and processed this word was an even greater desire to pursue revelation and breakthrough into one of the primary longings of humans: authentic community!

Through this time on the road our perspectives were greatly shifted, and we were challenged to enter into a new paradigm in many areas. However, it could easily be said that one of the most important shifts that took place was that we entered into a realm of commitment to each other that even outranked our commitment to an emerging vision. However, the result was not a weak vision but actually an even stronger vision than when it had been the primary focus. This was due to the fact that the vision was now being built on an essential substance of the Kingdom called relationship.

Divine DNA

Desire for this type of relationship is one of the primary longings of every human. Most of you care less about what you are doing and more about who you are doing it with. For the students who come through our training school, yes vision is desired, but even more than that they are looking for community with which to walk out vision. It is no mistake that God put this in the heart of a generation that would be a part of ushering in one of the greatest ingatherings of souls into the community of Christ! Not only is it naturally in the DNA of this generation to desire this, but it also happens to be one of the greatest keys to the release of the Kingdom. Throughout the Scriptures, as well as history, we see this principle lived out again and again.

Whether it was David and his mighty men, John the Baptist and his followers, Jesus and His disciples, or the early church in the upper room, history has always been marked when believers have gathered in true community centered on the presence of God. Scripture makes it clear that authority, power, and even maturity are released when two or three gather together and agree.

Again I say to you that if two of you agree on earth concerning anything that they ask, it will be done for them by My Father in heaven. For where two or three are gathered together in My name, I am there in the midst of them (Matthew 18:19-20).

Though one may be overpowered by another, two can withstand him. And a threefold cord is not quickly broken (Ecclesiastes 4:12).

And He Himself gave some to be apostles, some prophets, some evangelists, and some pastors and teachers, for the equipping of the saints for the work of ministry, for the edifying of the body of Christ, till we all come to the unity of the faith and of the knowledge of the Son of God, to a perfect man, to the measure of the stature of the fullness of Christ (Ephesians 4:11-13).

Community Defined

So what is authentic community? First I will tell you what it is not. It is not forced or fabricated. It is not just living in the same building. It is not feeding each others' insecurities or needs for affirmation. It is not just sharing the same values, and it is certainly not all agreeing on the same theology! In addition to these things, authentic community is also not lots of Facebook friends or full chat rooms or big contact lists in our cell phones.

Authentic community begins with God at the center of a group of people! This begins to morph into a group who have all died to their own ambitions, reputations, and preferences. This emptying of self-focus and selfishness is of absolute necessity to any true community. It results in a community that empowers and walks in power. This has been most exemplified by the love of the Godhead toward each other and toward humanity. It begins with the Garden, the cross, and the upper room where the greatest community in all of history, the Trinity, became incarnate that they could extend an invitation to partake in the love that is shared in their perfect expression of authentic community.

> *That they all may be one, as You, Father, are in Me, and I in You; that they also may be one in Us, that the world may believe that You sent Me* (John 17:21).

Authentic community becomes one of the greatest expressions of the Godhead and of the increase of the Kingdom of God. In the three greatest expressions of incarnation with man, we can see three of the most dynamic keys to authentic community.

The Garden

In the Garden, God walked with humankind. Humans had a choice of whom they would walk with, and for the first period of time in the Garden, they chose God. Walking with God necessitates a coming out of our own wills and desires and gazing at the One who created it all. The first key to authentic community has nothing to do with each other and everything to do with Him! He is the source and center of any move toward community and committed relationships. We miss this so often in our pursuit of corporate unity. It is not first and foremost about just trying to figure each other out and get more compatible. Surely that can help, but it will never go anywhere if He is not the primary focus of all of life, both individually and corporately.

The Garden represents both the intimacy and fruitfulness of authentic community because that is what the Father displayed by creating it and by the privileges He gave. Walk with *Me*, be fruitful, and multiply! The name of the garden, *Eden,* literally means "pleasure." It was Adam and Eve's mandate to take this lifestyle of walking with God to the ends of the earth. Even the names of the four rivers that flow out of the Garden speak of this purpose. In the order that they are stated in Genesis 2, the meaning of the four rivers is: "increase," "bursting forth," "rapid," and "fruitfulness." This could very easily be read as "increase bursting forth" and "rapid fruitfulness." This was always the intention. Fruitfulness through intimacy. Physical children are the fruit of physical intimacy. Spiritual fruitfulness is the result of spiritual intimacy. This is true of authentic community as well. And the primary emphasis that God the Father spoke through the humility of allowing humans to walk with Him was that this community, which began with Adam and Eve and would become millions, was always meant to be centered on Him!

What a humble God, who would allow Himself to be seen, experienced, and enjoyed by humans. This incarnational love of the Father and reciprocated focus of His people is the primary and first essential key to the beginnings, longevity, and fruitfulness of community. Without it we are simply humans trying to fix human problems and finite beings sitting around trying to figure out how to get along long enough to actually bring change to the world. The result is the forming of perhaps one of the greatest strongholds in human history: humanism. Humans as the solution to humankind's problems and the ultimate good that can bring change. It has never worked and never will work. All attempts at authentic community begin with the revelation of a God who loved His people so much that He invited them into the unity of the Trinity by an invitation to walk with Him in the Garden.

In addition to the focus of His Presence as the source of all unity, we cannot forget either that this focus necessitates an adherence and conforming to what He defines as truth. Without His truth, in the written Word, being the principles by which we all seek to abide, we will continue to live in a quagmire of relativism. This will result in a re-defining of truth and no community whatsoever. This is called anarchy and it is the opposite of community. So community must begin with a focus on *Him* as a person and Him as *Truth* itself in the Word that He has given to us!

The Cross

The second example of the three primary incarnations of the God-head is Jesus' life on earth, specifically His embracing of death on the cross. Once again we have the tremendous humility of God, this time through the life of the God-Man, Jesus the Messiah. Jesus, through His incarnation, established for us the second most important dimension of authentic community: selflessness! If the first mistake that we often make in our attempts at community is to try and find our source of unity in each other, then the second error that will inhibit us from step-ping into the fullness of what is possible is self-focus, self-protection, and self-absorption.

The greatest hindrance to any type of community setting, whether it be living in community, worshiping in community, or praying in community is our addiction to self. We are addicted to meeting our own needs, having things our own way, and protecting number one! Most of the time, the outpouring of the Spirit is held at bay because in times of corporate worship and prayer, we are rarely focused on Him, His desires, and even the needs of those around us. We want to worship our way and pray our way, depending on how we feel at the moment. If there is something I wish our whole generation would make their motto, it would be, "It is not about me." I personally believe that if we recover this one thing, we will stumble into the greatest revival in history! A revival of selflessness is the reviving of the first and second commandment that Jesus gave us. Love God and love your neighbor. This point cannot be overstated. We have swung the pendulum so far in this area that recovering the biblical truth is going to require many voices to be raised up with a message of the love of God unto true surrender of self-focus.

Jesus is the model. Dying to Heaven's bliss, the throne room, His absolute power, and His own comforts, He took on a body of flesh and the limitations of man. He went on to completely embrace the plan of the Father for the redemption of humankind, ultimately leading Him to the greatest act of selflessness in human history, the cross! *For I have come down from heaven, not to do My own will, but the will of Him who sent Me* (John 6:38).

Intimacy must eventually lead us to selflessness and the desire to not do anything except the will of the Father. Otherwise it is not true relationship but rather self-gratification. It is the same in our communities, friendships, and marriages. Why do most marriages end? Selfishness. Why do churches split every day? Self-focus. Why do most bands last only a few years, and many missionaries end up coming home after a few years? Personal agendas and an addiction to self.

The kind of selflessness that Jesus modeled starts by living it out in our relationship with God and then flows into our relationships with those around us. Imagine what would be possible in our corporate gatherings if everyone truly came with no thought of self. Imagine what our weekly gatherings of believers would look like if everyone came to pour extravagant love on God and each other. Imagine the community that could be experienced in any setting of the world if everyone came to the table with their self-protective walls dropped and actually were real! Imagine actually being known as you really are, or actually knowing those in your community as they really are. No more plastic smiles, no more fake responses, no more masks, but people living real, and yet not just seeking to meet their own needs in their vulnerability. It seems we either live with very little vulnerability at all or so much that all we can see is our weaknesses and issues and never have a thought of serving those around us.

Jesus beckons to every one of us to come and live the Gospel of selflessness, for there is no other Gospel. He set the example and we must follow if we are to enter into one of the primary longings of each of our hearts, authentic community!

The Upper Room

The third primary example of the incarnation was perhaps the greatest act of humility of all. In the Garden, God walked with humankind. In the life of Jesus, God became human. However, something entirely beyond human imagination comes to us in Acts chapter 2: perfect God, in the Person of the Spirit, fills imperfect man. No greater act of humility and incarnation could be walked out by God than to actually put Himself into vessels of clay still in the process of sanctification! In this act we have the third key to authentic community: empowerment. The Father came to set our priority on Him above everyone, establishing the true source of unity. The Son came to set the example of dying to self for the sake of the whole to teach the way of sustaining community. The Spirit came to inject Himself into our innermost beings, teaching us the ***power*** of community.

Empowerment only works in an environment of gazing at God and death to self-focus. If empowering others is the primary goal of community, we will quickly lose our focus. If community is void of empowerment, then we will quickly become enabling and passive rather than empowering and fruitful. This has happened throughout human history. Believers have gathered together to simply be together with no real purpose and no real empowerment. For the Trinity to fully invite us into the community God enjoys it took the risk of empowerment. In the same way, for us to walk in authentic community we must risk the failures and mistakes that will be made as we empower others. The opposite of empowerment is control. This spirit has also attempted to create community, and the result has always been loss of value, death, and dictatorship.

Imagine if in our churches, communities, and ministries everyone sought to bring out the strengths, and to fight for the destiny, of all of those around us. The competitive spirit in the Bride would be crushed, independence would be destroyed, victories would be celebrated, and everyone would move further and further in maturity and fruitfulness. Just as the Spirit took ordinary people and empowered them for extraordinary feats, so the Church living in the empowerment of those around us will result in a corporate authority and community power that we have historically called *revival* and *reformation*. This dimension of community is what leads to tremendous outward impact and growth of the Kingdom. We must learn to encourage the dreams on the hearts of those whom God has brought us into relationship with. We must rediscover the power of being a Jonathan to the Davids around us or a Barnabas to the Pauls and John Marks that come across our paths. Without Jonathan, who would have warned David away from Saul? (See 1 Samuel 20.) Without Barnabas, who would have fetched Paul after many years in obscurity? (See Acts 11:25-26.) Without Barnabas who would have empowered John Mark to be who God saw him as, eventually becoming useful to Paul, who would not even take him as a side kick earlier on? (See 2 Tim. 4:11; Acts 15:37-38.)

If we were all willing to walk a little more like Barnabas and Jonathan, we would see many more emerge as Davids and Pauls who, in turn, would release the Solomons and Timothys. However, when we all aspire to a place of influence, favor, or authority like we see in David or Paul, then we actually self-destruct the whole process of empowerment in community and end up right back in isolation, fragmentation, and independence.

Kingdom Come!

Authentic community is the cry of a generation, but are we willing to live in the example of the greatest community in history, the Trinity? Are we willing to intimately look to God and to Truth as He defines it as our source of unity? Are we willing to joyfully enter into a life of selflessness instead of self-focus? Lastly, are we willing to live a life that empowers all those around us to be the fullness of who God has called us to be? If so, you are ready for authentic community and ready to embrace the most fertile seedbed of Kingdom expansion and Kingdom growth the world has ever seen.

10

THE SCRIPTURES TESTIFY

The dream is communities centered on the presence of the Lord breathing revival and reformation into the atmosphere everywhere they go! Picture a generation walking in radical character, fiery zeal, transforming power, and intimate love. Believe in an army emerging from the coals of broken families, broken lives, and a broken society. An army that is ready for battle with their eyes set on the Lord of the armies of the hosts of Heaven. Living in urgency, dying for a legacy! Filled with the confidence of Heaven, the perspective of the angelic, and faith for breakthrough. Let the fire of God fill you even as you read these words that were always meant to be your job description, your name tag, and your resumé. We are a people of breakthrough! Lift your heads, raise your voices, take to your feet—you are an army!

Succession

The previous words could be used to describe any number of groups throughout history that have completely changed the world as we know it. We would be foolish to believe that this is a "new" thing that God is doing. This is the oldest thing that He has ever done. From the very beginning, God looked at Adam and said be fruitful, multiply, and take dominion over the earth. None of these words are defensive, for they all speak of a Kingdom moving, advancing, and winning! Be fruitful in all of life, multiply your fruitfulness, and let your multiplied fruitfulness spread over the entire earth!

As we look at the present and dream toward the future, it is important that we realize we are not birthing a new thing but rather carrying on a very old thing in godly succession. Here is the definition of *succession:* The coming of one person or thing after another in order, sequence, or in the course of events.[1]

Unless we understand succession, we are in danger of missing the bigger picture and moving in pride. We must understand the context of human history we fit into, the past moves of God, and seek to walk in our part of releasing the Kingdom of continuation in our day. It is as if we are part of a family business that dates back thousands of years. It will never come to an end but actually end up monopolizing the planet and all other businesses. But unless we know the history of the business, we are in danger of accidentally starting a new business or completely redefining the business rather than taking it into its next season while carrying the same family name, same family history, and same final goals.

Just as a business must change to accommodate the changes of trends, the economy, and the demands of society, so will the Kingdom and its manifestation take on many different faces and many different manifestations. However, the lineage does not change, the Boss never retires, and the goal is still the same. Certainly there will be unique ministries that are birthed and seemingly "new" ways to reach the lost or communicate the Gospel. However, the reality that we are part of a historic, current, and future Kingdom never changes. The history of this Kingdom will always be our history, the King of this Kingdom will always be the King, and the goal of fruitfulness that brings dominion will always be the goal. So the question is not, "What new thing does God want to do?" but rather, "How to do we carry the work of our fathers into the next season of human history?"

Well, first we need to know a bit of the ways the Father has moved in the past, learn from the principles, and allow them to manifest in our day in the way that will most impact society. The principles never change, although their outward working will.

Presence Prioritizing Heritage

All throughout history, there has been a radical remnant who have contended for, prioritized, and enjoyed the presence of the Lord above everything else in life. The results have always been dominion over the powers of darkness and a great release of the Kingdom of Light! There have been times in history where this flame-toting remnant has been a mustard seed in size, and yet it has always prevailed over even the most violent attempts of the enemy. God has always faithfully preserved His seed and this seed has faithfully endured the most difficult trials in human history to pass the torch onward.

The incredible reality about our day is that no longer can those who carry the seed of intimacy and mission be called a remnant. *Remnant* by definition refers to a small amount that remains. It would be inaccurate to call anything that is happening today a remnant! The historic remnant, in their faithfulness, has led to an army of devoted radical believers who literally exist in every nation on earth. Never in history has there been a day like ours where so many carry true zeal and deep regard for the presence of the Almighty as well as a hatred for sin! We are far from perfect and still a distance from the mature Bride that we will be, but *remnant* is not even close to an accurate word to describe this present phenomenon!

A Man Like Few Others

One of the original lamp stands of intimacy in history was the man David. Brought up in the fields with the sheep, he was the perfect candidate to redeem a broken, distracted nation to a kingdom whose true King was worshiped above all else. Many books have been written about David and his contending, prioritizing, and enjoying of the presence of God. But let us observe the difference between the kingdom of Saul and the kingdom of David to get a clearer picture of what God is doing in our generation and is ultimately after accomplishing in His Bride.

When Saul became king of Israel, the ark of God's presence had already been taken by the Philistine army and no longer resided in Israel geographically. It certainly was no longer central to the priority of the people! After wreaking havoc on the Philistines, the ark had been returned to Israel. However, it was so disregarded in society that it remained for many years at the house of Abinadab (see 1 Sam. 7:1).

Ichabod was written over the nation, meaning, *"The glory of the Lord has departed from Israel"* (1 Sam. 4:21). All during Saul's reign, we see Israel go through one struggle after another, many lost battles, fear of armies on all sides of them, and little or no regard for the presence of God. Saul ruled from the perspective of a societal king, trying with the size of his army to defend Israel and extend its borders but with little or no fruit. *Ichabod* certainly has to be one of the saddest statements to ever be written over a people who used to be led by the cloud by day and the fire by night.

We see a major transition in the paradigm of Israel when the shepherd and lover turned king assumes the throne of Israel. With David's ascension to kingship came his rich past with the Lord. Hours and hours of intimate discourse with the King of kings in the night by his sheep, years of hiding under the shadow of the Almighty as he ran for his life, and through it all, a deep regard for the reputation and glory of God to be reestablished in the life of His people. I tell you, God is raising up Davids even as these words are being written and read—men and women who will lose themselves in the reputation of the Lord of Hosts, whose primary priority in all of life will be His Presence, and whose longing will be to enjoy and release the glory of His Presence everywhere we go! Let your heart be gripped with the dream that gripped the young shepherd boy, the cave-dwelling vigilante, and the poet king. Set your heart and life to be a restorer of His glory to a world over which the enemy is desperately longing to mark "Ichabod"!

Dancing on Ichabod

Shortly into the reign of this king, who never knew whether to be king or a hopeless romantic for His God, he makes his way to the house of Abinadab to bring the true King back to Israel. After one failed attempt, David violently crushes the Ichabod accusation over his people as he foolishly and recklessly dances the presence of God right back into Jerusalem. Filled with fiery jealousy for the reputation of His God and an intense longing for "one thing" above everything else, David once again places the presence back into the center place that it was always meant to have! This same holy, romantic violence is filling the heart of a generation that will never be satisfied until Ichabod is struck from our nations and glory is released without measure as the Church contends for, prioritizes above all else, and enjoys with immense pleasure the presence and Persons of the Trinity!

The result in David's kingdom and in all of human history has been the dominion of God's Kingdom over the kingdoms of man. David's rule was no exception. With the cry of "one thing" on his lips, David leads Israel into one victory after another until peace is established on their borders and David hands his son a presence-centered, prosperous, powerful nation.

Now, thousands of years later, the covenant is different, but the principles are the same. Contend for an outpouring of His Presence, prioritize His will and desires above all else, and enjoy Him immensely. Dominion, influence, revival, and reformation will be the result! It is so simple and yet it seems so difficult.

Antioch's Wisdom

Acts 13 is an incredible biblical model of the early Church. But, before going too in depth with this example, let us set a context with Acts 2. The disciples were given a clear strategy by Jesus to wait on

Him until He poured out His Spirit. As that glorious day came, and His Spirit was poured out, the disciples were filled with world-shaking fire! As they walked out onto the streets, they became burning men and women who began to set others' hearts aflame. Before long, 3,000 more had given themselves to be consumed by the same fire! If you were one of these disciples, and you had just waited on God, been filled with fire, and saw 3,000 people saved, what would you do when you woke up the next day? Well, for the early church, they seemed to think this was a pretty good strategy. It only made sense for them to keep trying this same strategy.

Many summary statements throughout the chapters of Acts point to a lifestyle of prayer, teaching, community, signs and wonders, and the masses turning their hearts to Jesus (see Acts 2:42; 3:1-8; 4:23-31; 5:12-16; 6:4). Pray, get filled with fire, take it to the streets, and watch the masses come running. So when we arrive at Acts 13, this is not an isolated statement with no history validating what the disciples are doing.

> *As they ministered to the Lord and fasted, the Holy Spirit said, "Now separate to Me Barnabas and Saul for the work to which I have called them"* (Acts 13:2).

The church in Antioch is only continuing to do what had been working so well since Pentecost. They were prioritizing Him and ministering to His heart. From that foundation, the Holy Spirit speaks, they obey, and the result is a thriving move of God across the nations!

> *Then, having fasted and prayed, and laid hands on them, they sent them away. So, being sent out by the Holy Spirit...* (Acts 13:3-4).

Where did we lose this strategy? Have we become too smart or sophisticated or too politically correct? John Wesley had a similar strategy when he spoke to his followers saying, *"Catch on fire with enthusiasm and people will come for miles to watch you burn."*[2] This enthusiasm is not something we can put on in the morning like a religious smile but rather comes from gazing at Fire Himself. This life of gazing, enjoying, contending for, and prioritizing the presence and Person of Jesus was the key to the miracles, signs and wonders, and salvation.

This one little statement, *"Ministered to the heart of the Lord"* in Acts 13, I believe to be one of the primary statements we must return to if we are to walk in the fullness of the dreams of God for this era of salvation history. We must come back to the priority of ministry to the heart of the Lord. It may not feel like a productive task; we may not be able to check something off of our "to do" list at the end of the day; and it may not make for flashy newsletters at first or eye-catching Facebook bulletins. But I tell you it is the key to apostolic Christianity. Filling our hearts with the priority of being "with" Him, longing to gaze at Him, shaping all of life around Him, and from that place, releasing His earth-shaking presence wherever we go! The key is to restore communion "with" Him. Not the language of intimacy or the appearance of intimacy or the concept of intimacy, but hungry humanity in love with raw God.

It seems so easy for ministry to Him to take a backseat to the commissioning of people to "do" the work. Of course, we must do the work, but oh, to do it with joy, pleasure, power, and fruitfulness even in the hardest of situations and circumstances. The key to the hardest and darkest places on the planet is not more hard foreheads and harder workers. Though this is essential to fruitfulness, it must be built on lovesick hearts fascinated with the beauty of God and placing value in actually telling Him how beautiful He is. A tender heart is the key to longevity! In all of our hard foreheads and persistent work, we must be even more stubborn in our locked gaze, fascinated hearts, and verbal praises.

This communion naturally leads to a life that releases dominion—the marriage of missions and prayer. God communing in the Garden with Adam; Adam taking dominion of the planet from His communion with God. When the church comes back to ministry to the heart of God, revival comes back to the church. When revival is in the church, then the church transforms the world!

Endnotes

1. Dictionary.com Unabridged. Based on the Random House Dictionary, © Random House, Inc. 2009.

2. http://www.quotationsbook.com/quote/12614/. Accessed May 18, 2010.

11

HISTORY TESTIFIES

Patrick's Plan

In the fourth century, a man named Patrick tapped into this reality we have been talking about when he began a strategy for transformation based in the day-and-night singing of the Psalms to God. This strategy would carry the Celtic believers across the British Isles as well as northern Europe. Their message was birthed in intimacy and ministry to God, and that came with power, love, and tremendous fruitfulness. Through this movement, whole nations were converted to Christianity. Patrick's model was simple: (1) Build a community of believers right next to an existing community; (2) Begin to establish day-and-night ministry to God primarily through the singing of the Psalms; and (3) Go out into the community to develop friendships, teach basic education, feed the hungry, and preach the Gospel to the lost.

As they ministered to God, each region they settled in was altered in its spiritual atmosphere as praises began to fill the air! At the same time, their human hearts were kept tender and full of love. Out of this furnace, they actually had something to offer to a dying, pagan world, and the dying, pagan world actually wanted what they had! The most famous of these furnaces was located in Bangor, Ireland, where this model of ministry was walked out for over 300 years.

During this time, Bangor was known throughout the nations as the "light of the world." Thomas Cahill has credited these Irish believers, in his historical documentation of this time, as having saved civilization as we currently know it.[1] They accomplished this through their preservation of historical documents, books, and their educational programs.

Zinzendorf's Dream

The most familiar model of this marriage of missions and prayer is from Herrnhut, Germany, and the Moravian missions movement birthed there. In 1722, a group of refuges descended from the Hussites established a community in northeastern Germany named *Herrnhut.* This word means "the watch of the Lord," and the community became known around the world and throughout history as just that.

This movement of prayer and missions began on August 13, 1727, when the pastor of the community called for a love feast to celebrate the repairing of broken relationships that had come as a result of disagreements and squabbles. At the love feast, the presence of the Holy Spirit dropped with such intensity that it was later referred to as the Moravian Pentecost. The results were similar to the first Pentecost in the Book of Acts. Six days after the outpouring, the community began a day-and-night prayer "watch" under the premise that since satan was in continual accusation of the saints before God, how much more should the saints be heard before the throne of Mercy. This prayer watch would go on to last without a break for 100 years, and then after a short pause it resumed for another 20 years.[2] This all took place in Herrnhut, Germany. Other Moravian communities began prayer watches in various forms and lengths of time. This outpouring of the Spirit birthed a zeal for the presence of God that caused the believers to place His Presence at the very core of their society, work, family, church, *everything!*

After five years of day-and-night prayer, a young man named Alexander Dober had a dream in which he saw an African slave calling out to him for help. He became so moved by the dream that he appealed to Count Zinzendorf, the leader of Herrnhut, to allow him to sell himself as a slave to reach these slaves. This began a missions frenzy that would send out 1,000 missionaries over the next 30 years. This was more missionaries than the entire Protestant world had sent in the previous 200 years. The Moravians' intense focus on the presence of God, their faith in the power of intercession, and their zeal to reach the lost were more cataclysmic in nature than almost any single community or event in modern history.

Just look at some of the events that took place during these 120 years of intercession. The First and Second Great Awakenings rocked the world, some of the greatest revivalists in history lived, slavery in

England was abolished, Christianity became the core of American history, and the modern missions movement would move into full swing from every denomination and many missions societies. The world was literally changed! How much can be attributed to the Moravians? This question is impossible to answer, but it seems that a model of apostolic church was recovered in fully contending for, prioritizing, and enjoying the presence of God. As a result, a fire for evangelism ignited that set millions of people free.

The Layman's Prayer Revival

The last historical example that I want to point to as an arrow of faith for what God is doing today is the Layman's Prayer Revival. This is perhaps one of the least-known and yet massive moves of God in the history of American revivals. In 1857, a man named Jeremiah Lanphier took over the outreach ministry of a small church on Fulton Street in New York City. Church attendance was declining all over the city and for that matter over much of the nation. As Jeremiah sought the Lord on how to turn the tide in the city, he felt from the Lord to organize a one-hour prayer meeting over the noon hour. This was during the industrial era of America, and the majority of the working masses were involved in factory work. City whistles would blow signaling that it was time for lunch break. Jeremiah decided to call his prayer meetings during this lunch break.

In preparation for this, Jeremiah dispersed 20,000 flyers across the city hoping for a large turnout. However, on September 23, the hour came and went with only six people attending the first noon-hour prayer meeting. Jeremiah was not about to give up, and the following week when they had the next prayer meeting there were 20 in attendance. The week after, there were 40. This kicked off enough momentum that everyone agreed to move the meetings from a weekly event to a daily gathering. Little did they know what they were on the verge of seeing unfold.

Before long, 3,000 people were attending this gathering and another 3,000 meeting in Philadelphia and 2,000 in Chicago as well. The hunger for the presence of God grew to such a point in the cities of the United States that the work whistles began to blow at 11:55 and 1:05 instead of the traditional 12:00 and 1:00. This allowed everyone to have five minutes to get to and from the meeting, allowing for a full hour of prayer. At the height of this revival, it was said that it was almost impossible to find a shop that was open during the noon hour because everyone was at the prayer meeting. Imagine New York, Los Angeles, or any city in America basically shutting down because the entire city had such a hunger for God and such a longing to meet together in prayer![3]

We have gone through numerous dry spells in the church over the years. Many believers' primary experience in the area of prayer has been boredom. However, in our day, once again, God is pouring out the gift of desire on His Bride, and just like in Jeremiah Lanpher's time, we are growing in our hunger for the presence of God. This is leading to zeal-filled prayer even when it is inconvenient! All throughout history, there has been a remnant whose hunger for God drove them into being inconvenienced by their longing for more. These history-shaking prayer meetings often led to sleepless nights, cancelled university classes, and required long journeys just to get to the meetings. In these times our drive for success and finances take a back seat to desperation for the only hope and answer to all of the needs of humankind.

This is God's divine strategy for reaching the lost. Get filled with hunger for God, get filled with the fire that hunger draws, walk the streets, spheres, and nations as burning lamps lighting every dark corner with the light of life in the face of Jesus Christ (see 2 Cor. 4:6).

Prayer Frenzy

This prayer revival broke down every denominational wall as people were no longer concerned with getting to their particular church, but rather, they literally ran from their factories to whatever church was nearest. There was a literal frenzy to get as quickly as possible into the posture of prayer, as people never wanted to miss these intense, intimate times with God. The gatherings were inspired by the words of Jesus in Mark 14:37, *"Could you not watch one hour?"* This motivation led to an intense hour of prayer and fasting that spread like an out-of-control wildfire into every major city of the U.S. and even jumped the ocean to release a similar move of prayer and fasting in the British Isles.

The media became one of the primary ways that this move of God in New York began to spread. The editor of the *Herald Tribune* happened to be looking out his window one day when he saw thousands begin to pour out of the factories, fill the streets, and in a matter of minutes disappear once again into every nearby church. Curious of what was happening, he sent a reporter into a church to find out what all the visible excitement was about. The reporter came back to share that the churches were in prayer. Over the next days as the prayer gatherings continued to grow, this editor would send out his reporters all over the city to find out the numbers of those gathering. Over time the reports went from 25,000 to 40,000, and each time these meetings were reported it only caused them to grow more. Because of articles being written, many other cities across America began to hold similar meetings, and it quickly spread across the nation.

Just stop for a moment and realize what could happen with today's global communications network. Just last week, I was in Buenos Aires as part of a global 24-hour prayer day where at least 70 cities gathered from around the world synchronized for the same 24 hours of worship and prayer. We began and ended with a global conference call with many nations and cities represented. I was amazed to think of the power of global communication that is now available and how it will play a major role in this next move of God. Imagine what will begin to happen around the world as reports on YouTube, Facebook, Twitter, Internet news, television news, and cell phone technology begin to share about the dead being raised and thousands being saved, delivered, and healed! The testimonies of God pouring out His spirit on "all" flesh will be unstoppable. The result will be more outpourings, more faith, and more moves of God that snowball beyond man's ability to comprehend or control!

Testimonies of the power of God are one of the primary ways that God is going to prepare His Bride to be mature upon His return. These testimonies will carry so much authority and power that millions will not only give their lives to Jesus for the first time, but the sleeping church will wake up inspired by what God is doing all over the earth. The supernatural power of the testimonies upon those who see and hear will actually cause many to turn away from compromise, apathy, and sin as they are caught up in the fervor of a tidal wave of God's presence being poured out.

The testimonies of the Layman's Prayer Revival are powerful and far-reaching. The power of God moving across the cities was so tangible that even ships loaded with passengers were reported to have fallen to their knees in repentance before they even reached the harbors, knowing nothing of what was going on in the cities. By 1859, just over one year from the first prayer meeting at the Fulton Street Church, over one million new converts had been added to the church. Not Christians just moving from one church to another, but one million lost souls brought into saving knowledge of Jesus, fellowship, and discipleship! Just so that we can understand how massive this move of God was, let us compare the population of America in 1859 to the population today. One million souls coming to Christ in 1859 would be equivalent to over 16 million new believers in 2010. Imagine 16 million of the lost coming to salvation in one year! Is the church even prepared for a move of God like this?

Imagine the Possibilities

As the church began to prioritize ministry to God and prayer for just one hour a day, revival was released! What is possible as we rise up all over the nations of the earth with great desire for the presence of God and an unwillingness to do life, church, or missions without radically devoted hearts? This devotion will naturally lead to a lifestyle that will make great sacrifices to see the lost reached and the Kingdom released. We have no way to even measure what is coming. We cannot wrap our minds around it! As the Bride rises up in love and walks out His power, nothing will be able to hinder this unstoppable force. Let history remind us of not only the ways that God has moved in the past but especially the posture of the Church that birthed these moves! Let your hearts be baptized in confidence as we see that throughout history, God has poured out His Spirit through the praying, lovesick church and He is doing it again in our day!

Endnotes

1. Thomas Cahill, *How the Irish Saved Civilization* (New York: Doubleday, 1995).

2. Steve Addison, "The Morovian Missionary Movement" (September 1, 2005), http://www.movements.net/2005/09/01/the-moravian-missionary-movement.html; see also "History of the Morovian Church, "http://en.wikipedia.org/wiki/History_of_the_Moravian_Church.

3. Scott Ross, "Layman's Prayer Revival," CBN.com, http://www.cbn.com/spirituallife/churchandministry/churchhistory/FOR_LaymansPrayer.aspx.

12

URGENCY AND LEGACY

Throughout history it seems that the Body of Christ and society in general operate on a continual pendulum of overcorrection. We seem to always be responding to what we feel to be extremes. Instead of coming back to what the Bible points out as foundational and normal for all of life, we overcorrect and divide. This has led to massive division in the Body of Christ—and more denominations and non-denominations than can be named.

Not only do these splits, divisions, and overcorrections lead to the embarrassment of a seemingly schizophrenic God, but they also lead to a life that only partially reflects the Kingdom, the Gospel, and the King.

One such understanding that we have continually corrected and overcorrected, is the realm of walking in both urgency and legacy. Throughout history we can see different denominations, movements, and even societal trends that walked out either legacy or urgency almost exclusively. Those that have emphasized legacy oftentimes strongly focus on provision of a physical inheritance for their children, education of the next generation, and the health of the family. All of these things are completely biblical and true values of the Kingdom. On the other side, those that have seen life through an urgency-driven lens have often walked in tremendous zeal, stirred revival in the church, emphasized the salvation of the lost and the importance of milking the life out of each day. These values are also reflected throughout the Word of God and the life of Jesus.

Those camps that have emphasized legacy accomplished great things in the area of reformation, have had strong healthy families, have accumulated wealth that greatly advances the Kingdom, and have laid a strong foundation for a biblical worldview in areas of education and training. However, if this focus on legacy is lacking the dynamic of urgency, then sometimes, though biblically rooted, these individuals and groups may lack passion and zeal for breakthrough and daily intimacy with Jesus. Often risk is avoided for the sake of long-term gains. This can be good but can also lead to a generation that may have wealth and even understanding but that gives way to apathy. Sometimes these camps and individuals end up passing on a legacy of traditions based on principles that do work, but may not carry the life of the Spirit.

Those individuals who have a natural bent toward urgency or have grown up in groups with an urgency-driven way of life often really stir things up in the Body of Christ, press in to reach the lost, and carry a daily zeal to know God today and release His Presence on a daily basis wherever they may go. These people and movements naturally give themselves to great steps of faith that create the testimonies we all love to hear. Many times they are termed the movers and shakers in the Body of Christ. However, when legacy is not a part of an urgency worldview, families can be neglected for the sake of "ministry," character growth can be overlooked for the sake of power, and urgency can be short-lived and dwarfed in its impact because urgency did not think about legacy.

Balance?

This tendency toward overcorrection and division actually comes from a concept that may sound like it is opposite to extremism but in reality feeds that mentality. It is a concept called "balance." When it is not used according to its true definition, this word usually ends up being a foundation from which to define our own beliefs as balanced and define anyone who disagrees as extreme. For instance, if someone operates in the power of the Holy Spirit, the insecure, powerless Christian will point the finger and say that there is need for more "truth." For far too long the church has operated on a mentality of creating balances in all of life. And to a certain extent there are things that need to be balanced. However, much time and energy is wasted in trying to balance areas of our lives that scripture does not even call us to balance.

Have you ever heard it said that we need to live in a balance of Spirit and truth? It sounds great at first, but anyone who has tried to live this out or judge it in other people will soon find that it only leads to frustration and reciprocates the disease of "disagree and divide" that permeates the church today. The primary reason for this is that a balance of Spirit and truth is simply unbiblical. Just like most "balances" we preach, teach, or try to live, this is most often an excuse to emphasize what one person or group wants and to reject what they don't like. Then they go from protection of their personal comfort to criticism and judgment of anyone else who does not line up with their personal interpretation of balance.

The Fullness

However, what the Bible clearly teaches from cover to cover is a lifestyle of fullness. In the Book of Ephesians, Paul continually calls us to *"be filled with all the fullness of God"*; to be the Body, *"the fullness of Him who fills all in all"*; and to equip the Body so that we can walk in unity to *"the measure of the stature of the fullness of Christ"* (Eph. 3:19; 1:23; 4:13). Therefore, life is much more about receiving the grace to walk in the fullness of God and all that He intends for us than trying to pit Spirit against truth, power against form, faith against works, urgency against legacy, etc.

This thinking on fullness releases the liberty to walk in true equilibrium rather than overcorrection. Just as our inner ear contains a fluid that continually allows us to adjust to changing elevations and sudden movements, our spirituality becomes an embracing of tensions that will continually cause us to wrestle and draw near to the Lord and to learn to walk together as the fullness of Him who fills everything. Rather than setting our tent pegs in the camp that keeps us from having to confront insecurities, fears, and past wounds, we actually allow the truth of the Word, the leading of the Spirit, and authentic community to act as our equilibrium toward our growing understanding of the Kingdom and the ways of God.

Getting back to our topic of urgency and legacy, God is looking for a people who will not walk in the extreme of being completely urgency- or legacy-driven or in the so-called balance of urgency and legacy. Rather the fullness of God's desire for us is to be living in a daily urgency for a long-term legacy! This fullness is about marrying two ideas that were always meant to be completely embraced and in reality cannot function without each other. If urgency alone is my focus I will have no legacy. If legacy is my focus but I lack urgency, then my legacy will give in to apathy in the long run and not be a true Kingdom legacy at all. Instead, we are called to be radical in faith each day, carrying God's urgent heart to reach the lost, and walking in the daily zeal of a fire-filled relationship with a living God. We are to pour that zeal into our children as our number one disciples and into our spouses as our number one coworkers and partners. At the same time, we are to live filled with a longing and the action that will allow our urgency to still be fiery in 70 years. The goal is the marriage of urgency and legacy: the marriage of an urgent prayer life that lasts for 70 years and an urgent lifestyle of outreach that never neglects the long-term relationships in our lives. Urgency and legacy. Fire and fragrance.

Faith for Reformation

We are living in a day when conversation continually is thrown around about the current generation emerging from the Church being the last generation. This could be totally true—and certainly will be true of some generation. This kind of conversation does wonders toward a life of urgency, and it has been this way throughout history. However, history has already shown us the effect of a generation that got carried away in thinking of themselves as the "last generation."

A doctrine swept through the church in the early 1900s in regard to the rapture coming soon and the Church being taken out of a world that would later be destroyed. No matter your eschatology, this is a dangerous message to preach without walking in the fullness of urgency and legacy. What ended up happening has in many ways led to the degradation of at least one Christian nation: America. As this idea began to pervade the church more and more, Christians stopped getting educations, bringing innovation in the spheres of society, and influencing education, media, and the sciences. As a result, the influence of Christianity in the nation can get limited to Sunday morning services. Christianity usually ends up mocked by the media industry, voiceless in the sciences, and barred from education.

How did this happen? Aren't we called to be the light of the world? Aren't we filled with the most powerful and creative force on the planet? Aren't we called to lead in all areas? Yes! And we can once again, but we must not let our eschatology confine us to our own 30, 50, or 70 years on this earth. It is time to teach our children that in their urgency they must not forget their legacy. It is time for us to raise up a generation that, if God calls them to, will urgently posture themselves in 10 years of schooling so that their legacy can influence governments, Hollywood, universities, hospitals, and every other area of society that has pretty much been handed over to the minds of those steeped in humanism with an agenda to prove the Church and God foolish and nonexistent! At the same time, we must teach our children to also live with the constant reminder that Jesus is returning and our lives are unto that cause. Our legacy should never steal our urgency or our legacy will be irrelevant. Our urgency should never shoot our legacy or our urgency is dangerous. There is hope for reformation in the nations, and it lies in the paradigm of a marriage of the fullness of urgency and legacy.

Urgency for Character

Part of the emphasizing of legacy that God wants to release in the midst of the urgency in our hearts is the importance of developing radical and godly character in our longing for anointing and power. These two things must be pursued together! It is time for our most anointed leaders in the Body, those walking in radical signs and wonders, to also be our leaders with the highest integrity. At the same time, it is also right for our leaders with the greatest integrity to be pressing into the release of the power of God through their lives. It is time for a generation to emerge whose desire for God and desire to impact society naturally lead into a desire to get free from every hindrance.

No longer can we pray for the sick one moment and the next moment think it is OK to give in to an addiction to pornography. No longer is it OK to prophecy the heart of God over an individual and the next moment give in to excessive alcohol. Where are the burning ones who will love nothing more than God and hate nothing more than sin? It is time to rise up with radical power and radical character. We have had enough fireworks shows in the Body of Christ! However, this is not an excuse to say that we should stop pursuing the power of God. Better yet, let us pursue zeal, power, and the gifts of the Spirit at the same time as we develop character, integrity, and break all sin that would entangle us. Anointing is never an excuse for sin. Developing character is never an excuse to not walk in the power of God! We need both, the fullness, urgency, and the legacy.

13

THE CHARACTER THAT SUSTAINS REVIVAL

I stood on the top of a small hill overlooking the quaint little community of Herrnhut in eastern Germany. My heart was brimming over with vision as I thought back on the move of God that had taken place on this very soil. For 120 years, the Moravian community sustained a 24-hour prayer watch crying out for revival in the nations and a release of harvesters into the harvest fields. As we have seen, out of this furnace of intercession and this authentic Christian community came a massive missions force that covered the earth. By the time their leader, Count Zinzendorf, had died in 1760, they had sent more missionaries into the world than the entire Protestant world in the past 200 years. Prayer and missions had truly converged. The thought of it was filling my own mind with future dreams, ambitions, and visions as I stood gazing over where it all began.

I could see a massive wave of young people going to the darkest and hardest places on the planet with the light of the Gospel, prioritizing His Presence and walking in the power of God. I envisioned thousands of communities all over the world that would live in authentic, loving community and be agents of revival and reformation. These thoughts still exist and actually continue to grow in my heart and mind. However, in the midst of this grandiose vision, the Lord began to speak to me about something else.

"It wasn't their vision that impressed Me," the thought wisped through my mind like the cool morning breeze. "It wasn't their strategy that changed the world," came another gentle whisper.

The Heart of It All

As I continued this dialogue with the Lord I was struck by my tendency to so quickly overlook the real cause of the Moravian missions and prayer movement and to immediately begin to draw up plans, strategies, and visions in my mind. I almost broke into tears as I suddenly felt the overwhelming love and pleasure of the Lord for the men and women whose simple love for God had compelled them to the strategies that would lead to a powerful release of the Kingdom of God on earth. It didn't start with strategy or vision; it started with love!

The emotion of the Lord began to course through my veins as I felt His longing for a generation whose love would be so deep, whose character would be so strong, and whose perseverance would be so supernatural that the natural outflow of their lives would change the world around them! It was as if I was a ship ready to set sail on the perfect course, with lofty dreams, and the crew to do it all. And yet all the while the Lord was longing to just be on board with us, not to just send us off! I felt His heart crying out for lovers who would work, not workers who would try to love.

It was the heart of these men and women as they stood on that same hill 287 years previously that had changed the world. It was the heart of Count Zinzendorf who had encountered the Lord at a young age and wanted nothing more than to glorify his Lord. Love was the motivation! Love is the beginning of every move of God and every ounce of transformation. Vision is glorious, and God is full of world-changing strategy, but it must begin with love. Sincere, unadulterated love that produces a character that can hold the new wine that God is pouring out. Only then do we become vessels that can have world-shaking vision without the vision becoming the goal.

Philippians 1:9-11 says:

> *And this I pray, that your love may abound still more and more in knowledge and all discernment, that you may approve the things that are excellent, that you may be sincere and without offense till the day of Christ, being filled with the fruits of righteousness which are by Jesus Christ, to the glory and praise of God* (Philippians 1:9-11).

Without Wax

This passage leads us from a love that abounds in knowledge and discernment into a life that understands what is excellent and makes decisions that will lead to a life of sincerity and blamelessness until the day of Christ. Love leads to revelation that will lead to godly character. The word used here in Philippians for *sincere* is a term that was used to describe pottery that was "without wax." In biblical times, vessels were made of pottery. When a vessel would crack, rather than throwing it out, wax was melted and used to fill the crack so that it could still hold water. However, this vessel's strength was damaged each time a crack was filled in with wax. When examining a vessel to verify its true strength, it was held up in the sun so that the cracks filled with wax would be exposed, revealing if the pot was actually strong or only had the appearance of strength. A pot was said to be "sincere" if it had no wax.

Love, abounding in revelation, will invariably lead to a life that is without wax. Only vessels without wax will last the test of time and trials of life to carry the wine that God is longing to pour out in this generation. This wine will undoubtedly lead to the greatest revival in all of history!

For far too long we have sought to create character in a generation without creating fascination with "Character" Himself! We have tried to convince people to walk in godly character without first allowing them to be convinced in their hearts that a loving God wants to teach them how to live according to His nature and character. Fascination with this loving God is the motivation that leads to emulation. What we cannot afford is another ministry or anointed individual who has two good years of ministry, tons of verbal vision, and a stellar Website, but ends up like an amazing fireworks show: the display looks great for a moment but then fizzles out in another sad story of divorce, immorality, financial dishonesty, or scandal.

The anointing is *hot!* When the heat is poured out, the wax in our character will melt completely and destroy the usefulness of our vessel.

For far too long we have filled the cracks in our character with a false substance that looks good on the outside but can never withstand the heat that comes with anointing, influence, and even the backlash of the enemy. However, as Philippians reveals, this kind of sincerity can only be created from a continuous abounding love.

Love Is the Motivation

It was this love that filled my heart as I stood on the hill overlooking Herrnhut. A prayer flooded my lips:

> God, raise up a generation of lovers! A generation that will love You more than life itself, that will give their lives to simply love You! Lord, fill my heart with more love than vision, more character than ambition. But let my love and my character be such that I can carry the most fiery, red hot anointing You have ever poured out! And God, not just another Zinzendorf, or another John Wesley, or another George Whitfield, but a whole generation of wholehearted lovers whose love for You will cause every bit of false substance to be exposed so that when You hold us up to the "Son" it can be said that we are without wax! Only then can we contain the vision and strategies that You are longing to pour out in this day. And not just for three good years, not just for a flashy title or Website, not just to start a movement, but to contend for a movement to begin and be carried on and on until You return!

The question and subject of character can no longer be a little paragraph at the end of a book on power and glory. It can no longer be kept to short conversation in private. Anointing can no longer be an excuse for poor character. Godliness must become forefront in our message and our lives! But the topic of character can no longer be a list of dos and don'ts either! The question is not, "Is it OK for me to do this or do that?" The question is, "Who is God? Who is this God who loves me so? What is He like? What does He like?" This fascination will birth God-like character and melt false wax leaving us sincere and without blame, not to mention full of anointing, until the day of Christ. Let us hunger to this end!

Daniel

We enter into this abounding love, unto increasing revelation, which leads back to abounding love. The natural outflow will be the ability to discern what is best in life, or what is excellent. The choices made from this premise of love, revelation, and discernment will be the key to the mature Bride that Jesus will return for. The mature Bride is not going to emerge when we finally get the right discipleship model up and running or finally have such good accountability groups that everyone stops sinning. Maturity will be directly related to the increase of love through the increase of revelation of God leading to choices that result in maturity. Daniel was a man who understood and walked this out. Look at the words below used to describe Daniel by those who observed him:

- Gifted in all wisdom, possessing knowledge and quick to understand (see Daniel 1:4).

- Knowledge, skill in all literature, wisdom, visions and dreams (see Daniel 1:17).

- Ten times better than all astrologers (see Daniel 1:20).

- Counsel and wisdom (see Daniel 2:14).

- The Spirit of the Holy God is in you and no secret troubles you (see Daniel 4:9).

- Light and understanding and wisdom like the wisdom of the gods (see Daniel 5:11).

- Excellent spirit, knowledge, understanding, interpreting dreams, solving riddles, and explaining enigmas (see Daniel 5:12).

- They could find no charge of fault, because he was faithful; nor was there any error or fault found in him (see Daniel 6:4).

We would all do well to have this as the epitaph on our tombstones. However, if this is to be said about our generation, or us as individuals, we must begin to repair the disconnect between this kind of reputation and the daily discipline and lifestyle choices that it takes to develop these qualities. We cannot disconnect Daniel's outflow of integrity, longevity, and anointing from his life of committed prayer, fasting, and seeking.

God is longing to fill us with an accurate view of the spiritual disciplines and allow us to begin to experience boundary lines in pleasant places as David refers to in Psalm 16. I prophesy and declare that God is raising up a whole generation that will be known for both great exploits and uncompromising character—radical power and a committed life of extravagant discipline! These will become inseparable in this generation. The world will look on with amazement as a company of Daniels emerges on the earth and in the Church whose character is above reproach and whose life is full of anointing, power, and love.

Influence Through Purity

In Daniel chapter 6, we have the familiar story of Daniel being thrown into the lion's den. Many of us grew up watching this story on either a flannel graph, VHS, or DVD. The story has become so familiar that we can miss the power of it. David's enemies had to create a law that was not previously in existence in order to find something wrong with him. Daniel 6:3 says he *"distinguished himself above the governors and satraps, because an excellent spirit was in him; and the king gave thought to setting him over the whole realm."* It is time that the church walks in such a level of character and integrity that we are not just known as those who constantly criticize or condemn our leaders. But we actually confront godlessness with the purity of our lives and gain such reputation that we don't have to force our way into positions of influence. What if we actually got invited to rule over nations because of the "excellent spirit" that we walked in? Out of jealousy, Daniel's enemies could only come up with one solution to take Daniel's power and influence away. They talked King Darius into an idea that only he could be worshiped or petitioned for 30 days and that anyone guilty of breaking this law would have to be thrown into the lion's den to meet his sure fate.

Daniel was undeterred by this threat and immediately went to seek the Lord. That day he bowed down to the Lord three times as was his custom since early days. Now the full weight of this statement of Daniel's consistency, devotion, and discipline can only be realized when one takes into account that the early days of Daniel's life were many years in the past. At this point, Daniel has been in captivity for 66 years. If he was 15 when taken into captivity, then he would be 81 at this time. If he was 20 when taken into captivity, then he would be 86. Either way, he was no young man, and this statement bears the weight of a lifetime of radical devotion in a pagan kingdom. This resulted in the reputation and anointing that we now read about and admire. This type of life is not developed accidentally. We are deceived if we think that we are going to stumble into greatness or accidentally live a life of ever-deepening intimacy and ever-increasing power.

Pleasure-filled Discipline

David said it this way: *"The boundary lines have fallen for me in pleasant places, surely I will have a delightful inheritance"* (Ps. 16:6 NIV). He recognized the direct correlation between a life within God-given boundary lines and a delightful inheritance. For so long, we have separated discipline and pleasure, thinking one is punishment and the other is freedom to do whatever we want. However, we are moving to such a place that boundary lines are discovered to be pleasant. As we live in them, we find ourselves getting off the tracks of the Christian roller coaster of ups and downs into a life of pleasure-filled discipline. This will lead to a true and lasting inheritance full of eternal delight!

Do you think Daniel ever got to the end of His life and wished he had spent less time in disciplined prayer and fasting? Does anyone ever get to the end of their lives and wish they had spent more time watching television, gazing at a computer screen, or wasting time in pointless activities? Doubtful! This is not a legalistic statement by any means. I am referring to true pleasure and delight in this life and the life to come. A heart fully postured toward the things of God and the things of eternity. A life spent on the things that really matter. A life of delightful boundary lines resulting in a life of radical impact!

Riverbanks

This statement of David on "boundary lines" could be likened to a river with high riverbanks that are impenetrable even in flood stage. Rather than overflowing the banks, this raging river, flowing by high walls, will only cause the river to go deeper and deeper. If a river has weak or low banks, the result is a flood delta, which ends up being a mile wide but an inch deep. Unfortunately, this has been all too true of many ages of church history. Instead, through a life of focus and delightful disciplines, we can become a people living in the river of God's presence for 70 and 80 years and only going deeper and deeper in seasons of "flooding" circumstances or overwhelming torrents. It is time to build the disciplines of our lives high as we set ourselves into a deep life of prayer, studying the Word, meditation, lingering in the presence of God, solitude, silence, fasting, excellence in finances, a tight reign on our eyes and minds, and a heart that consistently gazes at the face of Jesus!

The key to this life is not to do it out of obligation or duty, because someone said to, or even to impress those around us. We have to come out of the thinking that says that the foundation of Christianity is for me to love God more and in order to express that I will just get more disciplined. In one sense, discipline is an expression of love. If our disciplines are simply us trying to love God though, they will always end in striving and burnout. The key is this: He loved us first! The very foundation of the whole of Christianity is His radical, unconditional love for His children. Only from this foundation can we begin to approach the disciplines and allow them to posture us for more revelation of love and a greater response of love. Let this reality sink in. If our foundation of Christianity is anything but His love for us, then we are susceptible to works-based Christianity. A better way is to wake up every morning in awe of a God who can love us no matter what has gone on or is going on. Discipline, focus, and godly character are organic responses to the astounding revelation of this love. From this place, we will actually see a generation walk in more radical discipline than any prior one, but it will not result in religiosity or blind duty. It will actually be one continual response to the love of God.

A New Standard of Maturity

It is my firm belief that from this foundation of His love for us, resulting in extravagant expressions of love back toward Him, we will see a company of people excel in intimacy, revelation, and fruitfulness. We will call it acceleration, though it was always meant to be normal. The maturity of our 18-year-olds in the spirit will start to look like that of a typical 30-year-old, and our 30-year-olds will start to look, think, and walk like a 50-year-old. I believe this to be true due to the fact we have set the bar for Christian maturity and fruitfulness so low that when someone really sets their hearts and eyes on Jesus and begins to walk out the natural lifestyle, we all take notice and comment on how much beyond their age they seem.

I believe what we have defined as radical is going to seem complacent compared to where we are heading. What we have called acceleration will become normal. Christian maturity will be completely redefined as a generation of 12-year-olds start to fill our pulpits and streets with the fiery word of the Lord in their hearts and minds. They will lay their hands on the sick and see them recover, pray for the dead and see them rise, speak to the possessed and see them set free! This coming move of God will see believers rise up completely convinced, enamored, and distracted by the beauty of Jesus and the love of God. At the same time, they will begin to walk in discipline and focus that other church people may call religious simply because it causes them to feel lazy and apathetic by comparison. These fiery believers will also walk in great exploits, supernatural compassion, and out-of-this-world wisdom! It will be a generation like Daniel, a generation that sets aside microwave Christianity for a journey of long gazing and high riverbanks.

14

LET JEHU RIDE

I n the first days of 2009 at the Burn 24-7 annual global New Year's fast, our national team felt a stirring to focus our prayers and attention on believing for a new plumb line of purity and holiness to be raised up across America. We began to dream, believe, and contend for that radiant and spotless Bride to emerge on the stage of history in our lifetime as has been prophesied and promised throughout the Bible. In spite of the widespread and rampant moral depravity of society in our day, we ignited faith-filled prayers and petitions for a plan of redemption to be released and for holiness and purity to be restored in a generation. As we embarked on this journey together, God divinely spoke an identical message to the hearts of our leaders in a single 24-hour period. The premise of this message was a summoning that this new move of holiness must first be ignited in our lives.

This sudden passion and pursuit was sovereignly laid on each of our hearts and confirmed through numerous dreams, visions, and words. In response, we spent countless hours in worship and prayer sets, on strategic conference calls and gatherings, and at our leaders' summits discussing how to practically implement this in our personal lives—before we even begin to take on a nation!

A new moral revolution of purity and holiness is coming on a generation longing to be cleansed and freed so they can be *"blameless and pure"* in a *"crooked and depraved generation"* as Philippians 2:15 (NIV) charges. A life postured in this place of consecration and purity will be the foundation from where God releases sustaining fire on the altar of our hearts. We are not after a short-sighted or "flash in the pan" movement of purity and holiness. But as we cultivate and implement this in our lives, homes and families, we are actually setting the standard and passing on a legacy of righteousness to our children's children. That by the grace God has given to us to walk in this calling, generations yet to come form our lineage would follow the example we set forth!

The Epidemic

This journey is fueled by the command from God in Leviticus 11:44 and later reiterated from the New Testament in First Peter 1:15: *"Be holy, for I am holy."* This command sounds pretty simple and rather straightforward, right? Unfortunately, many churches, leaders, pastors, and believers across the Body of Christ are somewhat hesitant to tread near the topic of purity and holiness because of all that this subject entails. Opening up this "can of worms" forces us to draw lines, create boundaries, and bring much needed definition to what this new moral revolution actually looks like. There are many opinions, books, methods, conferences, theologies, and ideologies to entertain us on this topic from so many different streams. As many of these are actually in direct contradiction to each other, how can we ever hope to arrive under a unified course of action to defeat the enemies of lust and perversion devouring a generation?

Besides this obvious dysfunction of disunity on the matter, I believe we are also afraid of beholding just how immense this epidemic is that is consuming the hearts of millions. Similar to scratching at the surface of a floating iceberg that is really a thousand times bigger underwater, this crisis is far larger than many of us believe. Many say the identical scope of lust has been here ever since Adam and Eve were banished from the Garden, while others insist history has never encountered such an assault of lust by the enemy on a people.

The real question carried heavy on the hearts of the valiant remains: is there still hope for a turnaround? Can evil again be defeated? Was the victory of the cross enough? Will the destinies of a generation bound in this heinous spirit be unlocked? Can a sexually charged culture wrapped in shame and disgrace truly become the "light of the world" once again? Can we individually experience a breakthrough that could lead to a corporate advance against perversion in our homes, churches, and communities? The words of promise in Isaiah 59:19 give us a beacon of hope within the mire of this cultural plague: *"...When the enemy comes in like a flood, the Spirit of the Lord will lift up a standard against him."* It is time for the standard to be raised up in our day.

An Example Revealed

A certain phrase began to circulate among our "burners" as we would talk and pray concerning the state of America during this crucial hour of history. Knowing full well that our nation is in the midst of her steepest moral decline in history, we believe drastic times call for drastic measures. The words that came up in conversations, prayers, and even spontaneous songs were: *It's time for Jehu to ride like never before across the nation!*

God began revealing a timely biblical example from which we could gain much needed revelation. The story of Jehu in Second Kings 9 began to give language to what many of us were feeling stirring in our bones. It was an example emerging in our spirit that gave us hope and faith for what God could do in our day. A holy zeal and righteous anger began to rise up in our souls against the strongholds holding back a generation drowning in lust, shame, perversion, and unbelief.

When Jehu, son of Jehoshaphat, came on the scene in Israel, Ahab and Jezebel were reigning supreme and the land was gripped with the spirit of idolatry, perversion, and wickedness. Instead of the prophet Elisha taking matters into his own hands, God gave him strict orders to anoint a king to be the divine solution. This fact is very significant in the story and revealed a complete paradigm shift for the nation. It was the dawning of a new day.

The Relentless Drive

A man from the company of the prophets found Jehu, anointed him with a flask of oil, and gave him the direct mandate from the

Lord to dethrone the house of Ahab and establish righteousness again in the land. After Jehu finally overcame false humility and shared what the prophet had spoken to his friends, they blew the trumpet and proclaimed *"Jehu is king!"* (see 2 Kings 9:13). A nonnegotiable key to moving into our callings with sure victory over the enemy is surrounding ourselves with voices of truth. As displayed by the example of Jehu's friends, we must immerse ourselves in covenant friendships that call forth the destinies, callings, and mandates from God over our lives. These will be people and communities that "blow trumpets" and prophecy destiny over us even when we are insecure and our hearts are filled with daunting unbelief. Jehu's friends were voices that propelled him forward into his calling and did not accept anything less. Right after this took place, Jehu then immediately departed to fulfill this mandate. He seems to have been characterized by driving his chariot "like a madman" as he chased down and cut off evil powers while establishing righteousness in their place.

Despite facing the powerful prevailing rulers and authorities who had previously put to death the righteous who had opposed them, Jehu was undeterred. The sheer boldness and fear of the Lord he carried demanded the attention of even the most wicked. He was relentless in finishing the job until every single member of the house of Ahab was forever destroyed according to the charge God had given him.

As to those who were in opposition to him, Jehu simply gave them an option. As seen in Second Kings 9:18, he commanded them to "fall in behind" and join him in his pursuit. A fire of zealous passion burned inside his soul for holiness to be established as the new standard and for the nation to turn back to the one true God with fear and reverence. This fervor manifested in a righteous anger he embodied that silenced critics, swayed top leaders to join the cause, dethroned principalities, and convicted the nation of her waywardness.

Because Jehu positioned his lifestyle, attitudes, and heart in the place of purity and holiness, God discovered a man who could come into agreement and alignment with His nature. It is our response to the command to "be holy as He is holy" that postures our hearts to receive what is on the heart of the Lord. In other words, the radical pursuit of holiness in Jehu's own life created the capacity needed to receive the fresh mandate God wanted to release on a generation. He became the mouthpiece God used to establish a new line of authority and rulership in that day. It all started from the place of consecration and a lifestyle that was truly set apart.

The Stage Is Set

We are in another Jehu-like moment across America and much of the rest of the world in this day. The spirit of Jezebel and the house of Ahab are ruling in virtually every sphere of culture, including government, sports, business, media, the arts, and even the church, to an extent. This should come as no surprise. Even the prophetic promise in Isaiah 60 warns, *"Darkness covers the earth and thick darkness is over the peoples..."* (Isa. 60:2 NIV). The spirits of pornography, lust, abortion, homosexuality, humanism, and perversion are choking out the destiny of a generation, and their voices of influence seem to grow louder and louder each day.

The standards of holiness and purity in the church seem the lowest ever as we continue to allow the culture's numbing drone of lust sway us into a state of mediocrity, powerlessness, and passivity. What is even far worse is that the church remains largely silent. The spirit of humanism has indoctrinated the West to empower men to "choose what is best," all while the church is working harder than ever to become "relevant" and practice tolerance. We have allowed the lines to be blurred on subjects dealing with abortion, homosexuality, and beyond while excuses and "conversations" are replacing irrefutable biblical foundations of absolute truth. We have lost the brilliant facet that distinguishes us from the rest of the world and causes us to stand out: holiness.

A haze of confusion has gripped society and caused people to dip into deeper places of shame, depression, and disillusionment toward God and the church. The current studies and reports of twenty-somethings struggling with pornography, homosexuality, depression, bulimia, and self-mutilation are at all-time highs. What can we possibly do to reconcile this sadness? Can we really believe for things to turn around in our day? Should we not aggressively fight against these prevailing powers for the sake of our children and children's children? Has the church lost her identity and calling of being set apart, a light shining in the darkness or a "city on a hill"? Does God have a solution to restore the moral fabric of the nations?

Kings and Co-heirs

I believe the position has never been riper for the Jehus of the hour to arise and fulfill their God-given mandate. The stage of history has been set for Jehu to ride forth! God always has an answer and a countermeasure that is facilitated through the activation of sons and daughters who demonstrate and release the realities of the Kingdom. These sons and daughters will shine without blemish brighter than the noonday sun.

God's divine strategy is not just to call the prophets and those in "full-time ministry" to be the solution that brings reformation. This was also the case with Elijah as he was the renowned prophet of his day.

Historically speaking, finding a solution to the major national crisis with Ahab and Jezebel fell heaviest on his shoulders. But God's response is to nominate and anoint kings in their place of authority to rise up and take a stand against injustice and anything that holds people back from entering into the freedom Christ paid for on Calvary.

Colossians 2:10 exhorts and reminds us that every believer has *"been given fullness"* (NIV). We must break out of an ungodly paradigm that every believer is not already fully equipped to become the solution and hope for the darkness flooding the world. It is so imperative to understand that Jehu was not a prophet or a priest but was an heir to the throne. This mandate and high calling from God goes out to all joint-heirs of Heaven to establish His Kingdom dominion in the land. This is in one accord with the prayer of Jesus in Matthew 6:10: *"...on earth as it is in heaven."*

We cannot allow disillusionment to harden our hearts and desensitize us in this critical hour. A standard must be raised up! Just as darkness is increasing over the earth and working to enshroud a generation, we must live from the reality of what Heaven sees taking place on earth. Isaiah 60 also promises that in the midst of the increase of intense darkness across the earth, that *"the glory of the Lord rises upon you"* and *"His glory appears over you"* (see Isa. 60:1-2 NIV). What an astonishing picture of light radiating off the Church that exposes and overcomes the darkness.

The Greater Jehu

Unfortunately, Jehu did not finish out his days strong and returned back once again to the sins of Jeroboam. But he was only a mere glimpse and foreshadowing of what was soon coming to earth in response to the widespread crisis of humanity. Jesus is our perfect example and the greater Jehu who carried this mandate to ultimate completion. This fulfillment took place as the works of darkness were destroyed, a Kingdom was established founded on righteousness, and mankind was ultimately freed from sin and shame to be eternally connected with the Father.

Moreover, Jesus flawlessly displayed righteous anger throughout His ministry on the earth. The most prominent example occurred on the day He was ushered into Jerusalem with shouts and songs of *"Hosanna in the highest"* and waving of palm branches (see Matt. 21). Upon reaching the temple, He took everyone by surprise with what happened next. Tables were overthrown, a whip was used to drive back peddlers, and money chargers were commanded to depart and suspend their defilement of the house of God. Jesus was setting the lofty standard for His Father's house being consecrated as "the house of prayer." This is the very scene that I desperately want to see replayed from the flat screen of history in Heaven one day! Upon viewing this sight and all the madness unfold before them, the disciples were noted as remembering the lyrics of David in Psalm 69:9, which states, *"For zeal for Your house consumes me, and the insults of those who insult You fall on me"* (NIV).

It is interesting to notice that the disciples did not remark that Jesus was simply angry and upset, but they recognized that His actions were birthed from a place of deep connection and devotion to His Father. Everyone was completely mesmerized by the holy and righteous display of zeal playing out before their eyes as Jesus was fully confronting the wickedness and compromise of His day. He was so moved out of deep love and compassion for the people enslaved in debauchery that He could not help but display His violent love on their behalf.

Likewise, we must arise with this resolution in our hearts to boldly oppose every area of compromise in our own lives and the lives of our friends. It will take a violent and assertive love after God to move us to forsake all other lesser lovers of our lives and tenaciously pursue Him. We must remember to be clothed with compassion and understand that our battle is not against people but against the principalities and powers enshrouding them. Lust and perversion are aggressive forces coming to thwart and abort God's purposes for a generation. We too must become aggressive in our spirits to wholly desire and seek after holiness and purity!

As recorded in Acts 4:33, the disciples began moving into a season of advancement and empowerment by the Spirit and a "great grace" was released upon them. This same grace is raining down on our generation and enabling us to overcome every addiction, scheme, and temptation of the enemy that would paralyze our hearts with shame and barrenness. Our good intentions and hard-line discipline are not strong enough to keep us pure, but we must receive the grace afforded to us by the cross to overcome. We cannot operate with any sense of victory outside of this "great grace." Just as He has overcome, so now we can overcome.

A New Zeal

Possibly my favorite line from this entire story of Jehu, and one that I have preached and taught from often in the past year, comes toward the end of the story. At this point, Jezebel had been thrown down, Ahab and his entire household was destroyed, but Jehu was riding harder, stronger, and faster than ever before. As he encountered an old friend named Jehonadab who came to greet him, Jehu invited him along the journey by saying, *"Come with me, and see my zeal for the Lord"* (2 Kings 10:16).

The external display of our inward transformation through consecration, holiness, and purity will manifest in a new and fresh zeal that will gain the attention of the world. People are naturally drawn toward individuals who carry passion and live for a cause bigger than their own lives. Whether it is in the worlds of the media, the arts, business, politics, or any other sphere of society, zeal and passion move and attract the hearts of people unlike anything else.

Authentic zeal rooted from a heart of purity will clearly broadcast the message of the Gospel without taint or selfish ambition. The world will no longer view the church and scorn its hypocrisy. We are moving away from Christian rhetoric that has only helped to mask over the deeper issues of sin binding the Western church in powerlessness against the evils of the day. The standards must be raised to a higher level as we endeavor to live a lifestyle that is beyond reproach as Titus 2:7-8 exhorts.

Romans 12:11 also summons believers to *"Never be lacking in zeal, but keep your spiritual fervor, serving the Lord"* (NIV). This sound of authentic zeal spilling out from a life of consecration is the unadulterated voice the world is longing to hear. It is a clarion call resounding the frequencies of life, faith, hope, and a higher calling of being set apart. Just as it was with Jehu, we are in a day where the fervent zeal from our lives will win the attention of even the hardest of hearts. They will run to see what is moving a generation to pursue such a God with reckless abandon.

MTV's Fascination

During the first year Burn 24-7 really began to explode across the nation of America and even spill over into Europe, I received an interesting phone call from one of the leading producers of MTV. By this time we had seen the flame of passionate and zealous vertical worship, prayer, and mission spread to over 30 cities from Tulsa, Oklahoma, to Fort Smith, Arkansas, from Virginia Beach, Virginia, to San Francisco, California, and beyond. Some of the cities were big and well known, while others were smaller and off the beaten path. However, hundreds and even thousands of mostly young teenagers and twenty-somethings on any given weekend were flooding into these furnaces scattered across America. Musicians, artists, poets, and lovers of God were often staying all night long just to gaze on Him and unleash their songs of devotion. He, in turn, began to reveal true identity and the beautiful destiny of a generation. The fire just continued to get hotter and grow higher with each gathering!

People came from distances far and near in eager expectancy to man their middle of the night shifts as the watchmen on the wall for their city. *Relevant* magazine and other publications wrote feature articles and shared the story of the rapid expansion of Burn 24-7, deeming it the early signs in a generation of "a moving trend back to God." It was organic, raw, messy, and lacked much if any organization, but God showed up every time we met in these humble furnaces and seemed to stay until the last chord rung out. Not only was this occurring across the communities of Burn 24-7, but countless other organizations, cities, and communities were experiencing a similar era of expansion and explosion as they facilitated 24/7 worship.

The senior producer at MTV, who shall remain nameless, was in absolute shock upon hearing the stories of what was taking place. During our initial phone conversation the MTV people were somewhat dumbfounded. They were seeking after real answers as to why this phenomenon was taking place. It was hard for these "experts in culture" to grapple with the idea that young people would forgo weekend parties, beer, sex, drugs—and most of all, MTV's featured weekend television programs—to waste time praying and worshiping God! They barely even believed me that our worship leaders and musicians practiced abstinence and even went on extended fasts from food and different types of media. They hounded me with questions on what was drawing in this massive crowd from America's cities every month to pray and worship for 24, 48, or even 72 hours. I simply explained to them that an entire generation is truly hungry to experience the authentic presence of a very real God.

Then it was my turn to butt in with a few questions of my own. I began to ask them why they contacted me, how they even heard about this grassroots movement (we did not even have a Website at this point!), and how they got my cell phone number (which still kind of creeps me out). They began to explain that MTV had been doing in-depth studies, surveys, and working hard to discover habits and trends within their viewers in order to find new marketing strategies for the coming year.

The producer reluctantly informed me that for three years in a row, a poll had been taken from their viewers revealing something astonishing. The online questionnaire, taken before the beginning of the new program season, asked the viewers what they desired to hear and see more of during the upcoming season. For three years running, the answer overwhelmingly remained the same. This topic was surprisingly not a scandalous Britney Spears video, another reality show based on who slept with who, or even more juicy details on celebrity gossip. The viewers were demanding to know more about the true and living God! Doesn't that just blow your mind away?

Because of this consistent and perpetual hunger, the producers and filmmakers were forced to discover the "underground" communities and movements that were feeding this craving. Somehow and in some way, they stumbled onto the Burn movement and were eager to know more. They remarked that the name alone drew them in deeper. We almost even struck a deal that would have allowed an extensive camera crew to come and film an entire 24-hour Burn experience in one of our cities and air it as a segment on their show! The plans and timing fell through, but our contact and conversations remained for several months longer.

There is something about the passionate pursuit after God and the posture of holiness that is appealing, attractive, and perplexing to the world around us. Rather than trying to blend in to society, look really cool, and become "relevant," the eyes of the world are searching for a different example—one of authentic passion, zeal, and sexual restraint. They cannot seem to get enough of it. The early signs of a moral revolution are already upon us! Let this story cause faith to explode in your heart and cause you to believe that the world is watching your pursuit after purity.

It's Time to Ride

We are being summoned forth into a lifestyle of radical purity and holiness in our day. This will be the defining mark of a generation and what will position our lives to sustain the greatest move of God to ever touch the earth. Many will refuse this invitation to become transparent and acknowledge their lack. Some will even attack and mock this pursuit and label it as a move of "dead religion" that is not relevant to society. We must, however, continue to effectively disclose that the root of this push for personal purity can only come out of the overflow of deep and intense passion for the man Jesus. From this place, a genuine love will grow in our hearts to "be holy as He is holy" while witnessing to those entrapped in the entanglements of the world that they can be transformed the same way we are.

The cry of our hearts is to be consumed by the All-Consuming Fire. We want to be in the place He dwells, experience the fullness of what is promised us, and burn bright with a pure, unadulterated flame of love, purity, and devotion until the day we depart to be with Him forever. The verse in Isaiah below has never been more noteworthy to guide us along this journey. Let it be the charge and mandate for a generation of burning hearts all across the world!

> *...Who of us can dwell with the consuming fire? Who of us can dwell with everlasting burning? He who walks righteously and speaks what is right, who rejects gain from extortion and keeps his hand from accepting bribes, who stops his ears against plots of murder and shuts his eyes against contemplating evil—this is the man who will dwell on the heights, whose refuge will be the mountain fortress. His bread will be supplied, and water will not fail him. Your eyes will see the King in his beauty and view a land that stretches afar* (Isaiah 33:14-17 NIV).

Oh God, we ask that You would awaken a generation bound up in the schemes, sin, and perversion of Jezebel and cause us to burn for holiness as You burn! Call forth Your Jehus of the hour to arise with boldness, clarity, purity, and singularity of heart for the day that is upon us. Let them model and release this fresh and attractive zeal for the house of the Lord that moves a generation to restore righteousness, justice, and worship in every nation of the world. For it truly is the hour to ride and burn "like a madman" and dethrone every power and spirit of Jezebel and Ahab while enthroning the King of kings across the land!

15

THE GIFT OF HUNGER

An explosion of raw longing is rising in the hearts of sons and daughters awakening across the globe. It is the fuel to this violent pursuit we run after the purposes and dreams of God's heart for a generation. What is this longing? What is the desperation? Why has radical fasting, unending prayer, and reckless abandonment in worship become so widespread and rampant from the slums to the suburbs? Is it mere hype, grandiose emotionalism, or some super spiritual fad? Or is a true and authentic heavenly grace upon a generation in this hour? I believe it is the simple, honest, and unhindered cry for MORE!

As I travel across the globe visiting many different communities and cultures in many nations, I have witnessed something truly remarkable. I am blown away beyond measure that a company of people exists in almost every city and are truly beginning to push farther, deeper, and higher than what they have ever experienced in the past. They are the "rumbling remnant" and the "sound from the underground" releasing a roar of change from the status quo. They are forerunners, pioneers, and contenders living, breathing, working, and loving from a place of deep desperation. They are the dreamers. They are the history makers. They are filled with faith from the secret place. They are reaching for a greater measure of breakthrough for their families, cities, and nations. This drive for more is causing them to sacrifice and lay down everything and "lose their lives" as they know them to gain it all.

Many of us have experienced a small taste of a greater realm of glory, have been captivated with the deeper place of encounter with Him, and have allowed that experience to transform our lives in virtually every way. We are ruined forever for anything other than the fullness, and those "appetizers" have enticed us to press in for the full-course meal ahead! These moments of Heaven breaking in have set us on a course of violent pursuit after His face. The grace is being released to run harder, faster, and press in longer than ever before. During nearly every gathering I have been involved with in the past year, when the presence of God fills the room, people simply do not want to leave. It is not uncommon to end our gatherings literally forcing people outside the building to lock up while they want to stay and soak in every last drop of glory! Our meetings are not short, either—many of them last throughout the night and even for days! I absolutely love how God begins to invade our churches, ministries, programs, and prayer meetings and we no longer have to coerce and try to manipulate people into staying longer. Don't you feel exhausted from that? In some cases, the

Western church has worked too hard in trying to fill this void of true hunger with more lights, smoke, relevance, tolerance, humor, craftiness, and concerts. I believe it is time we give our meetings back to the Holy Spirit just like the New Testament church did in the book of Acts. Similar to the gatherings of the First and Second Great Awakening, a day is coming where we will have to turn people away even five hours before our corporate worship gatherings begin because there are too many hungry hearts to accommodate. We will simply allow their gut-wrenching desire for *more* draw them in deeper.

The European Journey

A few months ago, I returned from possibly the most rigorous yet wonderful journey of my life. The Lord gave us a clear word to gather a team of young skilled musicians, prophets, intercessors, and revivalists to converge on the continent of Europe for a six-week-long journey to stir the hungry. The mandate was to release a sound of awakening and life on the cold barrenness of the continent. We were commissioned from Heaven as "prophets of hope" for the hour. Just like the Lord sent Jahaziel to Jehosaphat in Second Chronicles 20:14-15 as the armies of the enemy were rallying against him to exclaim *"the battle is not yours, but God's,"* so we were sent to relay the same message to the burning hearts across Europe. The strategy in Jehoshaphat's day is the same strategy as today: the atmosphere of throne room worship truly releases victory.

A team of 11 firebrands traveled with me to six nations and we ministered for 32 days in a row at one point without a day off! The trip was exceedingly exhausting, yet so unbelievably fruitful and full of wild and beautiful testimonies. Our team was humbled and awestruck by a raw surge of hunger rousing across the continent. It was overwhelming and astounding to us as almost every single night was completely packed with leaders, pastors, worshipers, musicians, intercessors, and artists longing for more of God. Many people came by car or train from cities that were over ten hours away! That is a monumental inconvenience for Europe and not commonplace by any means. Whether it was a conference center at maximum capacity with 5,000 screaming worshipers in Holland or a post office turned into a prayer room crammed with 50 people in Wales, every night there was a heavy demand placed on Heaven to respond to the hunger of God's people. We witnessed creative miracles and healings, salvations, heavenly encounters, and moments where we didn't know if we could literally behold any more glory because we might explode!

There Is Always More

When I finally returned home from this epic expedition to briefly catch my breath for the next trip, I found myself caught in a daze. I was staring at the ceiling in my house, utterly exhausted. During those days on the tour, I drove the team and all our gear from city to city in an oversized, gauche 18-seater minibus. I navigated across highways and roundabouts while trying to remember to drive on the left side of the road. During the nights, I facilitated all the gatherings, including leading the bulk of the worship, preaching, and helping release impartation.

Every ounce of my energy, sound, and revelation for the hour had been poured out over the continent during the past six weeks, and I had nothing left to give. I was pondering back on the memories and the moments where God changed, rearranged, and invaded our plane, train, and bus rides, as well as the communities that were marked, rekindled, and set ablaze during our visit. Deep encounters with God's glory flashed back in my mind as I recalled the nights I was literally stuck to the floor by the thick weight of His Presence. As I reflected in my house that day during that moment of utter exhaustion, the Holy Spirit whispered something in my ear that was so tender and gentle but absolutely provoking to the core of my being.

He said, "Are you still hungry, Sean? Because there is always more."

At the frequencies from these words, my entire body went numb and was flooded with such a zealous passion that rose from some hidden reservoir of my soul. I began to crumble into a pile on the ground and weep before the Lord, asking Him for the gift of hunger to keep pressing on. I prayed violent prayers and contended over my spirit, my family, and the Burn 24-7 grassroots army across the world to not allow fatigue, exhaustion, and familiarity to breed forth apathy, complacency, and comfort in our lives and our ministry. We have to remain hungry, desperate, and ravenous for His Presence! There is always more, and it will never be possible to exhaust the resources, energy, and revelation of Heaven. There is an abundant supply available whenever we need it!

China's Move

One visit to China last year and two weeks of hanging with the legendary underground church completely blitzed my heart with a fresh cry for the gift of hunger to grace my life. I had heard the stories of the exploding move of God's presence in the nation, despite the widespread and immense persecution. Even the most conservative statistics reveal that over 10,000 lost Chinese per day are coming to Jesus! This modern-day movement far eclipses any historical account of widespread salvation during any other revival in history! How about that truth to break doubt in our hearts and silence unbelief? This has been anything but a quaint and contained move, but the eruption of the Kingdom of God has shifted the Chinese culture, including their government, and has reshaped that entire region! Once the epicenter of communism for the world, China is being transformed into a hotbed for revival.

The measure of breakthrough the Chinese are experiencing and walking in has released faith, hope, and perseverance into the heart of the Church around the world. This current move is a sign and wonder that a similar breakthrough is soon coming to other nations bound in intense and long-standing darkness. It has also further proved that not a single nation, stronghold, government, or boundary can keep out or hold back the move of the Spirit. He is an All-Consuming Fire that will light up everything in the way!

Beijing Blast

So what is it about the church in China, India, Nepal, and other places where the Gospel is advancing in unheard of dimensions? Does God love them more than the churches in the West? Has He already passed Europe by? Did America already experience her best years during the First and Second Great Awakenings? What is the key ingredient that distinguishes and sets the move in China apart? These were the questions burning in my heart as I journeyed over looking for answers. It all became increasingly clear to me on August 8, 2008, in the capital of China, Beijing. Actually, it slammed me like a ton of bricks and was an encounter I'll never forget for the rest of my life!

The nations of the world were gathered in Olympic stadium to commemorate the opening ceremonies of the 2008 Olympic Games. It was clearly the biggest single event in China's modern history, and the strength of their booming economy, their ever-expanding military, and their seemingly "diplomatic" society was on display. The entire world was invited to peek behind the communist veil for a few weeks. There were over 100,000 armed troops in strict and tight regiments on virtually every main artery of the city. They had such a grip on this bustling metropolis of 15 million people that a person could not even cross the street unless the armed military deemed it a warranted action! It was one of the craziest and somewhat scariest things I've ever seen!

About six months before the trip, I had an intense vision that included a charge from the Lord. This mandate was to help mobilize a regionwide burn and gather lovesick worshipers from across the nation of China to release a strategic 24-hour "strike" of worship and prayer. This was to take place in perfect sync with the lighting of the Olympic torch in Beijing. So here we were on this day of new beginnings on 8.8.8. We were hidden in this underground "cellar" room with no view of the outside and two separate hidden entrances.

Face to Face With Raw Hunger

There was no ventilation, air conditioning, or circulation of any kind in the room as hundreds of ravenous lovers were releasing a fragrance of worship and pouring out their finest on the feet of Jesus. It was hot, sticky, stuffy, sweaty—and the most beautiful worship gathering I have ever been part of to date. Pastors had traveled from as far away as the Mongolian border to be a part of this strategic gathering. A few of them had even "visited" a prison cell multiple times on their way to the capital city. One pastor remarked that staying in a cell for up to a week was not uncommon on these trips. Because of this, he left two weeks early just to make sure he would arrive on time! What a concept! Many people in the West forgo a church service or prayer meeting if the weather is just a little bit rainy. But the hunger and desperation from these underground burning ones is causing them to risk even their lives for a corporate moment of agreement in the rich presence of God.

This posture and sacrifice is so attractive to God that He cannot help but visit them and move on their behalf! At the same moment as the largest television audience in history at 4.7 billion (70 percent of the global population) watched the lighting of the Olympic torch on worldwide television that night[1], our team was hunkered down with hundreds of these Chinese warriors in an underground building on the outskirts of the city. We were igniting our flame of love and passion to God that would call His attention to the city as the world peered in.

Exposure of My Own Heart

I was slotted to lead the opening set for the night and kick the whole gathering off. However, I had quite a problem that night in my mind. I did not know hardly any Mandarin and was wondering how I would be able to lead them, as virtually none of them spoke or understood English. I thought that launching out on a few chords and singing out "Yesu" ("Jesus" in Mandarin) and "Hallelujah" (same pronunciation in all languages) would be a good start. I hoped this would last me the entire two hours of my set. What I failed to realize is that there is no such thing as "leading worship" with these burning Chinese hearts! One strum of the guitar and they could have cared less what I was singing or playing. They were lost in the place of throne room worship and "caught up" in the beauty, splendor, and holiness of His face.

I have never witnessed such instantaneous pursuit as the entire place erupted in loud praising, rejoicing, and weeping, and many even fell prostrate in the presence of the Lord. I have never been more convinced by a group of worshipers that they were genuinely in love with Jesus than by those in front of me that night in Beijing, China. This one encounter with them transformed my life. The Lord spoke to me that this component of raw hunger was what distinguished the church in China and was the core element to why He was moving so powerfully on their behalf.

A sober reality dawned on my heart. I had to accept that these people were simply hungrier for God than I was. As harsh and judgmental as that may sound, this proved so true in my life that day. My lack of passion, hardness of heart, and the mundane "routine" of ministry was exposed as a cover-up for the true longing for God that they possessed.

I recognized my lack in their presence and fell to the ground in a puddle of tears asking God to awaken this in my life and grace me with the same gift of hunger the Chinese church was carrying! This is what takes place when we begin to model our lives from the place of raw hunger. It has its way of exposing every fraudulent cover up or excuse that we could muster up to disguise the true longings of our hearts. Something was infused into the DNA of my spirit that day and I have never been the same since.

Asking for the Gift

Without this gift of hunger being released in our lives, we don't even know what we are missing! There are depths and levels of God that can only be accessed through raw longing to know Him more than our titles, schedules, boxes, comforts, and religious ideas. King David is a perfect example of a man who had so much blessing, provision, power, wisdom, and favor on his life—he had it all by earthly standards! What more could a man of his stature desire? But he continued to posture himself in a place of hunger. He is quoted in Psalm 84:2 as saying, *"My soul longs, yes, even faints for the courts of the Lord; my heart and my flesh cry out for the living God."*

David carried a heavenly revelation that the Spirit of God is attracted to and responds to our cry of hunger. I believe this was the very revelation that caused him to be called "a man after God's own heart." This caused David to be dependent on every word that came from the mouth of the Father and not to rely on his own ability, gifts, and performance but to seek His face afresh and anew every day.

We Are Starving

We are a people living in a day where we are more in need than ever for the manifest glory to reside in our midst. In these days, we cannot simply rely on our good theology, concepts, and strategies—we need and must have *Him* show up! He is a God that desires to be experienced and not just read and talked about as we often encamp around the stories of the past.

A great pioneer and trailblazer of the faith, Heidi Baker, shared with me recently that she spends one-third of her life pouring out and ministering to the church of the Western world. She said that she had no desire to spend so much time with a people she felt already had so much while the rest of the world had so little. (Statistics reveal that 95 percent of all of the resources for Christianity lie within the borders of America alone, even though it only contains 5 percent of the world's population.) Then she was brought into an open vision that changed her entire ministry paradigm and allowed her to see the true reality and a new global perspective. The vision was of a malnourished and emaciated child dying of starvation with a massive belly full of parasites. Above the vision were words that read "The Western Church." The saddest part of the vision was that the emaciated child did not even know it was dying.

This vision adequately represents the reality we have been witnessing across the Western nations during the last few years. People are literally starving in the midst of a consumer-crazed, pop culture, media-driven society. Even though we seem to have all the resources, books, and prophetic words right at our fingertips, the only food that can satisfy is the bread of His Presence. That is what we are lacking in our churches, services, homes, families, and cities. In the past, we thought the church and even the lost desired our flashy programs and glittery agendas. We really believed that they were the "tools" to draw in a disillusioned generation to comfortably hear more about God. What is becoming more apparent in our day though is that we are all really starving for a divine encounter with the very Person of God. Even the lost are searching high and low, spending billions and trillions, going to and fro, all to find a love that will not fail them. The hunger is growing and building as creation is truly longing for Him!

Remember, He is a God not just be talked about but to be experienced! We are witnessing an astounding amount of hungry hearts flood into our sessions of 24, 48, and even 100 hours of nonstop fiery worship, prayer, and presence from all denominations, backgrounds, ethnicities, and walks of life longing to "feast on the abundance of His house" and drink deep from the "river of His pleasures" (see Ps. 36:8). It is beautiful how sitting at His feet in worship is our identity and the single common denominator and "language of the Spirit" that brings us together in unity around this pursuit. Genuine hunger is drawing us deeper into the place of encounter.

Today, allow that gift of hunger to rise up in your spirit and lead you on this beautiful pursuit for the face of God! Ask the Holy Spirit to release this grace on you to go deeper, higher, and farther with Him in the place where He dwells. Even if you do not feel it right now, let the Lord expose this cry that resides in every human heart as it guides you into the deep depths of God. There is an endless reservoir of resources, vision, passion, guidance, and endurance in the place of His Presence. We just have to stay hungry and ask for it. He is more than willing and able to grant the desire of our hearts as Jesus promises in Matthew 5:6, *"Blessed are those who hunger and thirst for righteousness, for they shall be filled."*

Endnote

1. www.multichannel.com/.../134614-Beijing_Olympics_ Sets_Gold_Standard_4_7_Billion_Global_Viewers.php.

16

IT'S ALL ABOUT FIRE!

A s we close this book, we want to leave you with one word…
FIRE! Not just hype, not charismatic rhetoric, but raw fire!
The human heart filled with fire, a life that releases fire everywhere it goes. Throughout the Word, twice we are given an image of Jesus as a Man with blazing fire in His eyes. As we continue to grow in deep intimacy with Jesus, that fire in His eyes becomes our one consuming passion. Our desire is to behold His glory and receive the passion in His heart. It is the same passion that took Him to the cross, the passion that conquered the grave, and the passion that will bring him back to His glorious Bride at the end of the age for the wedding supper of the lamb, face-to-face intimacy! The fire from His eyes will spread to our hearts and begin to burn up all the chaff that competes for our

attention and affections. As the chaff is burned up, what remains is a heart, mind and life completely devoted to Him as Lord!

Burning Hearts

Two men walked down the road in deep dialogue concerning the events of the last several days. As they continued on their journey, a stranger approached them and asked them what they were talking about. To their astonishment, this man seemed ignorant of the recent happenings in Jerusalem surrounding the death of a prophet named Jesus of Nazareth. To their even greater bewilderment, this man then began to explain to them more about this man Jesus than they had even known themselves! Their excitement over their newfound friend and the company they enjoyed led them to coerce this man to stay with them for the night. As they sat down to enjoy a meal together, they began to break the bread, and at that moment their eyes were opened to see the true identity of who was at their table. At the exact same time, Jesus miraculously vanished! In total shock, they looked at each other proclaiming, *"Did not our heart burn within us while He talked with us on the road, and while He opened the Scriptures to us?"* (Luke 24:32). My paraphrase would read something like this: "How in the world did we not realize that it was Him? Nobody else makes our hearts burn with fire the way that His Presence does!"

Global Awakening

We believe that we are in the midst of a global corporate awakening to the presence of Jesus and that our hearts are starting to burn like never before. The testimonies and stories you have read in the previous chapters are a few examples out of millions that further confirm this truth. Familiarity, mediocrity, and life as we have known it are no longer enough. Even what we have defined as radical will seem apathetic compared to the Spirit of wisdom and revelation striking our hearts like lightning and igniting a fire that no water can quench and no river can wash away. A generation is emerging on the earth right now in the vein of the great men and women of God throughout history who have operated in the history shaking intimate, zealous knowledge of God and for many of them even unto death. This vein has existed throughout history and is exploding in our day in such a way that "righteous remnant" does not even do justice to the size of this global army. No longer is it 100 prophets hidden in a cave like during the days of Elijah (see 1 Kings 18:4), but millions of fire- and faith-filled believers inhabiting the villages, cities, and nations of the earth!

Business as usual will not cut it any more. Jesus did not die for a Sunday morning gathering or a tidy Christian club. He died for fire! He came to the earth to bring fire as spoken in Luke 10:49 but the earth was not ready. When He left the earth, the ground was prepared, and then the fire fell! For 2,000 years now, fire has been spreading across the nations. Today we live in the days of increase like no time in human history! Even as I write this, I sit at our little tabernacle of worship and prayer on the YWAM Kona campus with the sound of lovesick, hungry believers adoring God and crying out for more fire in their own lives than ever before. Oh, our hunger is for so much more! There must be more! Is that not the deep cry in every one of our hearts? It is the cry of His heart. Now is the time! What are we waiting for? Fire has come! Fire is here! Let's allow ourselves to be consumed!

As you have now read the stories, encounters, and concepts that have guided us along this journey deeper into the All-Consuming Fire, we now challenge and invite you to begin to practically implement and run after this dream in your life. Joining a thriving community of worshiping missionaries would be incredible and give you an instant connection and support on this pursuit for more. Burn 24-7, YWAM, and countless other organizations, communities, and churches around the world are a great ignition point. They provide excellent training, mentoring, and support to champion this cause in a generation. A consecrated and focused season of pressing into God will help in creating a foundation that will cultivate a lifestyle that can last a lifetime.

Still, many of you are called to pioneer this dream where it currently does not yet exist and where there may not even be a remnant already assembled. This could be in the jungles of Borneo, Indonesia, the arid desert of Yemen, the Himalayan Mountains of Bhutan, or the neighborhoods of Beverly Hills. God is summoning a people who would worship in Spirit and Truth into every unreached people group on the earth. He is also pouring out the provision, grace, and relationships to turn the dream into reality. He guides where He provides. This is the walk of the road less traveled, but yet a fulfilling and necessary journey to see the Kingdom of Heaven established on the earth!

Jesus commissioned us to spread fire to the ends of the earth before He ascended to Heaven. There is no nation, tribe, tongue, mountain chain, social sphere, or hidden crevice of the earth that is safe from this inferno being released from the burning hearts of a generation. A good place to start would be to ask yourself some serious questions: What is God calling you to long-term? What are you so passionate about that you would be willing to die for it? What do you fall asleep at night dreaming about? What sphere, region, or cause has God etched on your heart?

It can't stop here though. You need to then begin to ask the questions about these dreams becoming reality. What are you sowing your time, energy, and money into in order to get there? What are your priorities in this season to be walking toward the high calling on your life? Are you willing to take the risks that are always required to see the Kingdom released?

Identity, purpose, and mandates are not discovered just in books, sermons, or ten-step programs, but first and foremost in being with Him and hearing His voice where creativity, revelation, and an "Open Heaven" atmosphere is always available. Proverbs 29:18 warns us that *"Where there is no revelation, the people cast off restraint"* (NIV). It is the revelation of being with and beholding Him that will cause us to lose even our very lives for the sake of love. This dream of living a life centered on His Presence must become our reality if we hope to bring any transformation to a dying world. His Presence is the lone strategy for the hour and where all the strategies, healing, restoration, breakthrough, and guidance will flow. We must be a people in this season who cultivate a lifestyle of living, breathing, and working from the place of His Presence. Since friends of God will always make the best workers, striving, performance, and working to gain attention and affection must decease in our lives. We are left with no choice but to simply surrender to His love and allow it to burn us deeply.

In His Presence, His dreams become our dreams. In His Presence, our motivation to bring His Kingdom is released from a place of intimacy. As this happens, **go!** Be obedient! Keep it simple! What is God saying? Do it! Walking out the dreams of God becomes one simple step of obedience after the other. Hear His voice and step out! There is a cause worth living and dying for!

We declare that we have been crucified with Christ and we no longer live, but Christ lives in us. The life we now live, we live by faith in the Son of God, who loved us and gave Himself for us! Oh God, we count all things rubbish compared to the surpassing greatness of knowing Christ Jesus, our Lord! Oh God! Raise up a generation that is radically in love with You, totally surrendering to you, and completely abandoned to Your purposes.

Our prayer is that this simple book and its simple stories and teachings would be a motivating fire that fills your heart with revelation and faith for what we are on the verge of. Let it feed the fire that already exists in your heart! Allow it to cause you to find your place on the wall, your place in the Kingdom, your fire and your fragrance!

More About Sean Feucht

More About Andy Byrd

DESTINY IMAGE PUBLISHERS, INC.

"Speaking to the Purposes of God for This Generation and for the Generations to Come."

VISIT OUR NEW SITE HOME AT
WWW.DESTINYIMAGE.COM

FREE SUBSCRIPTION TO DI NEWSLETTER

Receive free unpublished articles by top DI authors, exclusive discounts, and free downloads from our best and newest books.

Visit www.destinyimage.com to subscribe.

Write to: Destiny Image
             P.O. Box 310
             Shippensburg, PA 17257-0310

Call: 1-800-722-6774

Email: orders@destinyimage.com

For a complete list of our titles or to place an order online, visit www.destinyimage.com.

FIND US ON FACEBOOK OR FOLLOW US ON TWITTER.

www.facebook.com/destinyimage   facebook
www.twitter.com/destinyimage   twitter